EXTENDED SCIENCE

Diseases and Disorders

Selected Topics

P T Bunyan BSc MIBiol

STANLEY COMPREHENSIVE SCHOOL,
TYNE ROAD,
STANLEY,
CO. DURHAM.

Stanley Thornes (Publishers) Ltd

© P.T. Bunyan 1984

All rights reserved. No part* of this publication may be reproduced, stored in a retrieval system or transmitted in any form or by any means, electronic, mechanical, photocopying, recording or otherwise, without the prior written consent of the copyright holders. Applications for such permission should be addressed to the publishers: Stanley Thornes (Publishers) Ltd, Educa House, Old Station Drive, Leckhampton, CHELTENHAM GL53 0DN. UK.

First published 1984 by
Stanley Thornes (Publishers) Ltd
Educa House
Old Station Drive
Leckhampton
CHELTENHAM   GL53 0DN

*An exception is made for the word puzzles on pp. 6, 14, 47 and 72. Teachers may photocopy a puzzle to save time for a pupil who would otherwise need to copy from his/her copy of the book. Teachers wishing to make multiple copies of a word puzzle for distribution to a class without individual copies of the book must apply to the publishers in the normal way.

British Library Cataloguing in Publication Data
Bunyan, P. T.
    Diseases and disorders.—(Extending sciences; no. 3)
    1. Pathology   2. Medicine
    I. Title   II. Series
    616   RB111

    ISBN 0-85950-109-4

Typeset by Tech-Set, Unit 3, Brewery Lane, Felling, Tyne and Wear.
Printed and bound in Great Britain by Bell and Bain Ltd., Thornliebank, Glasgow.

CONTENTS

Chapter 1   What is Health?

Activity 1 Keeping healthy	5	Tapeworm wordfinder	6

Chapter 2   Internal Diseases — Microbes at Work

Being ill	9	Vaccination against disease	12
Activity 2 Bacteria growth	10	Questions on internal diseases	13
Ways of controlling microbe-caused diseases	11	Wordfinder on microbes	14

Chapter 3   External Diseases and Parasites

Psoriasis	15	Skin parasites	18
Seborrhoea	16	Question on parasites	21
Warts	16	Crossword on skin diseases and parasites	22
Ringworm	17		
Athlete's foot	17		

Chapter 4   Acne — A Teenage Worry

Skin	23	Activity 4 Adverts	31
Skin structure	23	Activity 5 Problem page	32
Acne	24	Activity 6 A shy friend	32
Activity 3 Experiment to investigate the grease-removing properties of soaps	31	Questions on skin	32
		Crossword on skin	33

Chapter 5   Hair — A Growing Problem

What is hair?	34	Activity 8 An investigation into dandruff shampoos	39
Hair growth	35	Activity 9 Perming and dyeing	39
Hair care	37	Questions on hair	40
Dandruff	38	Crossword on hair	41
Activity 7 Experiment to test the abilities of different shampoos to remove grease	39		

Chapter 6 **Cancer — A Major Malfunction**

Forms of treatment	45	Wordfinder on cancer	4
Questions on cancer	47		

Chapter 7 **When Parts Fail**

Heart diseases	48	Diabetes	5
Activity 10 Surgical problems	50	Wear and tear	5
Activity 11 The heart	52	Questions on parts failure	5
Kidney failure	52	'Heart transplants'	6

Chapter 8 **Social Diseases**

Smoking	61	Sexually transmitted diseases (STD)	6
Drinking	64	Questions on social diseases	7
Obesity and anorexia	65	Wordfinder on social diseases	7

PREFACE

This book considers some of the aspects of health that may confront a teenager today. It is not written as a manual on how to remain healthy. The topics have been chosen because they are of interest and not always easily found in biology textbooks. Acne and hair problems are often extremely important to teenagers. I have tried to explain them in such a way as to lay to rest the many myths which surround them.

Topics such as heart disease and cancer may not seem immediately relevant, but the phobias and misconceptions which surround them can often arise through lack of knowledge. Many children, too, will come into direct contact with these diseases through relatives, and indirectly through reports by the media. They are therefore important and years of teaching have shown that children are often anxious to know more about them.

This book will find its place alongside many biology courses at third, fourth and fifth years. It can be used as an addition to some of the major topics in these courses. Its information is interesting and relevant. It may be used as a basis for class discussion or for homework with the inclusion of the end-of-chapter questions.

Throughout the book I have attempted to keep the language simple and it is my hope that children will find it easy to read as well as interesting.

P T Bunyan
Roade School, Northants

ACKNOWLEDGEMENTS

The author and publisher wish to thank the following who provided photographs and gave permission for reproduction

Dr J M Boss, Skin Department, Gloucester Royal Hospital (pp. 15, 16, 17, 29); Paterson Laboratories, Manchester/Cancer Research Campaign (pp. 44, 45); Philips Medical Systems (p. 46); Imperial War Museum (p. 7); Department of Nephrology, Southmead Health Authority (p. 53); Public Health Laboratory Service (p. 34); Hugh Rushton (p. 38); St. Bartholomew's Hospital (p. 66 upper); Thorn EMI Ferguson Ltd (p. 1); Mrs Fay Titterton and Weight Watchers (p. 66 lower)

The word puzzles are by Don Manley of ST(P)

CHAPTER 1
WHAT IS HEALTH?

Most people understand what is meant by 'being in good health'. Being healthy is the normal condition for most people, most of the time, but what exactly does it involve? Our bodies are very complicated structures made of many parts, each with its own job. As long as each part performs its job correctly at the right time, then we are healthy. Being ill generally means a breakdown in the correct working of one part or another.

It is difficult to imagine the extremely complex way in which the many parts of our bodies work together. Even the largest factory producing, for example, specialised electronic equipment, is less complicated than the body. What is more, the body does it with far less fuss than you would

A modern factory

expect to find in a factory. At any one time your heart is beating, your lungs are taking in air; you may be walking down the street, whistling a tune, thinking about your dinner. At the same time your gut is digesting breakfast, your muscles are using energy to make you move, your brain adjusting your body temperature and your eyes taking in information about what is going on around you. These are only a few of the things that your body does. If any one of these jobs is not done correctly, then you may not be as healthy as you should be.

There is a lot happening in this body

To be healthy the body needs food, water, oxygen, exercise and regular rest. Anything which interferes with the proper supply of these may make us ill. For example, to remain really healthy it is necessary to have a *balanced diet*. This is to say, you need the correct amount of protein, carbohydrate, fat, vitamins, minerals and roughage. *Proteins* are necessary for growth and repair of damaged cells; *carbohydrates* and *fats* give us energy and keep us warm. *Vitamins* and *minerals* are needed in tiny amounts to keep the body working properly. Too much of any one of these is wasteful and unnecessary (and in the case of many vitamins, can be harmful). Too much fat and carbohydrate may be very harmful, as you will see in Chapters 7 and 8. Too little food of any sort leads to deficiency problems; for example, too little protein means you may not grow as well as you should. If any of the vitamins and minerals are missing from the diet, then particular deficiency diseases result. You can read about these in most biology books.

An unbalanced diet produces an unhealthy body

Health can be affected in other ways. We could be infected by a *microbe* of some sort, a small animal or plant which enters the body and begins to grow and reproduce. Microbes may use our food or sometimes feed on body cells, killing them and causing damage to our tissues. Some microbes not only use our food but produce substances called *toxins* which are poisonous to our cells and may kill them. Microbes are much smaller than human cells.

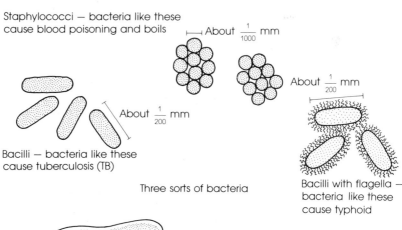

Different sorts of microbes

Staphylococci — bacteria like these cause blood poisoning and boils

About $\frac{1}{1000}$ mm

About $\frac{1}{200}$ mm

Bacilli — bacteria like these cause tuberculosis (TB)

About $\frac{1}{200}$ mm

Three sorts of bacteria

Bacilli with flagella — bacteria like these cause typhoid

Entamoeba — a one-celled animal which can cause dysentery

About $\frac{1}{20}$ mm

We could also be infected by larger organisms which we call *parasites*. Some of these, like the tapeworm, live in the intestines and use digested food before the body has time to absorb it. The tapeworms feed and grow while the infected person grows thin. Tapeworms are extremely rare in the United Kingdom but other worms, like the threadworm, which are not particularly harmful, are quite common.

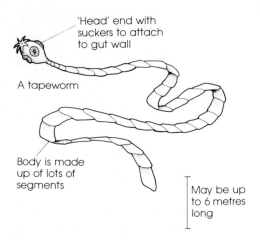

Parasites which can affect people

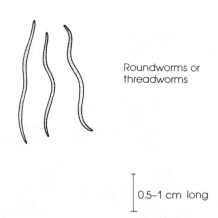

Parts of our body may break or wear out, possibly because we have failed to look after them. Broken bones are often quite easy to mend, but replacing the heart, liver or kidneys is not so easy. Our lungs can become filled with dust and smoke and simply not leave enough surface area for oxygen to get into the blood. As yet, lungs, like many other parts, cannot be replaced.

We could become ill simply because of the way we live. Staying up late, not getting enough sleep, taking hurried meals without giving our bodies time to digest the food properly can all put a strain on the body. If done for long enough, this strain is bound to damage something. Being healthy, therefore, involves not only avoiding harmful or damaging things but also looking after what we have — treating our bodies with some care and respect so that they last as long as possible.

With something as complex as a body, there are many ways in which it can go wrong. By understanding some of the problems which can arise, you will be in a better position to maintain a healthy body. There are many more things which can go wrong than you will find in this book. You should realise too, that the same part of the body can stop working properly for many different reasons. You may know of a situation which is slightly different to the one explained. You may feel that either you, or this book must be wrong. This is not the case at all. It just shows how complex a healthy body is.

While you read about the sorts of problems which can arise, you must remember that for most people most of the time, their bodies work pretty well.

SUMMARY

You do not have to be 'ill' to be unhealthy. As you will see in the following chapters, for example, your skin can be unhealthy but you would not consider yourself ill. Remember, to be healthy you need the correct food, and enough water, oxygen, rest and exercise.

ACTIVITY 1

Keeping healthy

EITHER:
Draw some cartoons to show the five things that the body needs.

OR:
Design a poster to draw people's attention to the things they need to stay healthy.

OR:
Write about the ways you keep yourself healthy.

TAPEWORM WORDFINDER

Do not write on this page, copy the wordfinder on to a piece of paper.

By following the clues below see if you can follow along the length of the two separate tapeworms. Worm 1 starts in square 1 at the bottom and finishes in square 1 at the top; similarly Worm 2. As you solve the clues you can move one square at a time in any direction, including diagonally. Each answer follows on from the previous answer and the worms cross each other twice. To help you, part of Worm 1 is shown shaded.

M	A	D	E	N	S¹	H	A	S²	K
L	Y	T	I	H	A	E	A	L	D
N	E	M	U	P	M	O	G	O	T
R	A	N	O	D	W	T	R	A	W
T	E	C	A	R	O	N	G	O	E
H	I	A	T	R	O	N	O	H	E
M	R	V	V	A	E	I	N	E	R
O	W	G	U	T	F	C	H	P	U
O	I	O	O	U	E	R	N	O	T
N	N	R	Y	T	E	E	D	H	G
G	P	R	E	T	H	O	O	T	I
N	A	R	A	E	D	N	S	F	R
O	E	E	H	W	I	S	I	U	N
R	G	G	Y	T	H	N	I	I	F
W	A	W	Y	M	O	F	A	V	E
N	Y	X	C	O	R	R	O	H	A
E	Y	N	O	B	B	A	I	N	D
A	G	A	I	S	E	L	D	E	E
T	R	O	G	O	A	C	N	D	A
T	A	N	O	C	S	D	L	O	C
S	S	U	U	S	A	U	U	S	I
T	E	L₁	N	G	U	M₂	S	T	O

Worm 1

1 Organs which take in air (5)
2 One of its jobs is to adjust your body temperature (5)
3 One of the things you need to remain healthy (4)
4 Another thing you need to remain healthy (5)
5 A substance which gives us energy and keeps us warm (3)
6 They are needed in very small amounts to keep the body working properly (8)

Worm 2

1 These use energy to make you move (7)
2 A gas necessary to keep you healthy (6)
3 Food necessary for growth (7)
4 An organ which can be replaced if it wears out (5)
5 Taking these hurriedly can, after a long time, help to make us ill (5)

6

CHAPTER 2
INTERNAL DISEASES – MICROBES AT WORK

Most microbe diseases are caused by *bacteria* or *viruses,* although occasionally fungi and single-celled animals, called *protozoa,* are important. Microbes cause disease by using our bodies as a means of reproducing themselves. In doing this,

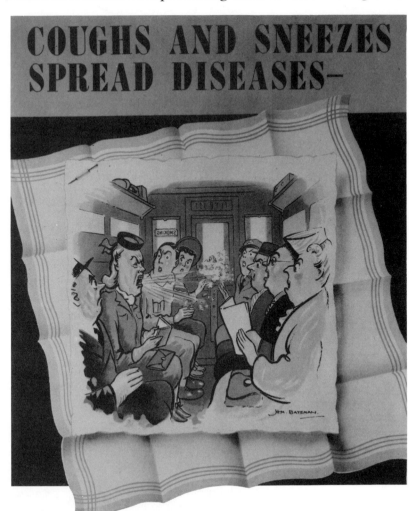

A war time government poster

the microbe may consume body cells as a source of food or may use the food that our cells need. Often the problem is not the cells which are lost but the poisons, or toxins, which the microbe makes and releases as a normal part of its life processes. These toxins are chemicals which interfere with the chemical reactions which normally take place in your body and which you need to stay healthy.

Microbes consume cells and produce toxins

Your body is well equipped to deal with microbes. Your blood contains different sorts of *white blood cells*, whose job is to find and destroy anything which is not part of your body. These white blood cells cluster around any sites of infection.

Phagocytes feed on, and digest, microbes

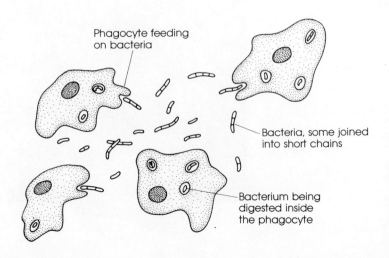

There are several kinds of white blood cells. *Phagocytes* actually feed on microbes and digest them, as shown in the diagram. *Plasma cells* make chemicals called *antibodies*. Some of these attack microbes and cause them to break up. Others cause microbes to stick together so they can be more easily destroyed by phagocytes. Others react with the toxins and make them harmless. These are called *anti-toxins*. *Lymphocytes* also make antibodies but instead of releasing them into the blood like the plasma cells do, they carry them to the microbes. The lymphocytes actually touch the microbes and use the antibody to make them break up.

Plasma cells and lymphocytes recognise microbes by the presence of different chemicals called *antigens* on the microbe. This, as you will see later, is important to medicine.

BEING ILL

You may wonder then, why it is that you become ill. This is principally a matter of numbers. First the microbes have the upper hand and then the white blood cells multiply until they are in the stronger position. Microbes are able to reproduce very quickly. Some bacteria will, in the warmth of your body, reproduce by dividing into two, once every half-hour. This means that if only one bacterium gets into your body and starts to reproduce, then in half an hour there will be two. Half an hour later there will be four, and so on.

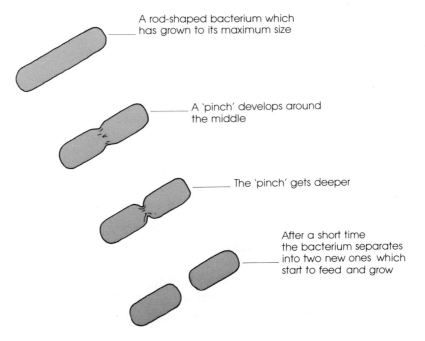

A bacterium reproducing

ACTIVITY 2

Bacteria growth

Copy out and complete the table below for the growth of bacteria.

Time (hours)	0	0.5	1.0	1.5	2.0	2.5	3.0	3.5	4.0	4.5	5.0
Number of bacteria	1	2	4								

Now draw a graph to show the increase in numbers of bacteria using your figures. (Do not write on this page.)

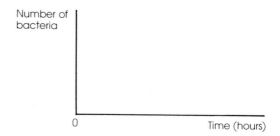

As you can see, in a very short time there may be enormous numbers of microbes. They reproduce so quickly that the white blood cells are unable to cope and the disease gets out of control. The speed with which the microbes can multiply is the reason why you can become ill quite suddenly and quickly. In response, your body starts to produce more white blood cells but this takes time. It also takes time for lymph cells to manufacture antibodies. During this period you are ill.

While you are ill, apart from feeling unwell, you may have a higher than normal temperature. This increase in body temperature is caused by the effect of the microbes on the white blood cells. Gradually the numbers of white blood cells increase. More antibodies are produced, which helps the white cells kill the microbes more effectively, and the disease comes under control. Your temperature falls and you return to normal.

A microbe-caused disease can be divided into three time periods. The *period of incubation* is the period when the microbes are multiplying and during this time you do not have any symptoms of the disease. This may last hours or weeks, depending on the disease. Even so, in most cases, the transition between being well and being ill does not take very long, because the microbes multiply enormously in number. The *period of illness* is when the disease has control. The *period of recovery* is the time when the microbes are being destroyed. The length of time for each of these periods will vary.

Some diseases caused by microbes

Microbe	*Name of disease*
Viruses	Measles Mumps Smallpox Chickenpox Polio
Bacteria	Tuberculosis Tetanus Pneumonia Blood poisoning Whooping cough Typhoid

WAYS OF CONTROLLING MICROBE-CAUSED DISEASES

To lessen the effects of diseases, and in some cases to prevent death, many drugs have been developed. These often work by attacking and destroying the microbes, and are called *antibiotics.* Antibiotics are only of use on bacteria-caused diseases. A bacterium is a cell which needs to feed and obtain energy like any other. It can be killed by interfering with its life processes. A virus is a very small particle which needs other cells to multiply. It has few of the normal life processes of a living organism. All viruses do is penetrate living cells and make them build new viruses. Even bacteria can be penetrated by viruses. Because they are so simple, viruses are very hard to kill: antibiotics which will kill bacteria, are no use against viruses. In many cases the treatment for a virus disease involves reducing the symptoms that the patient feels. The destruction of the virus is left to the white blood cells.

For this reason you may go to your doctor feeling ill and come away with nothing more than advice to take aspirin. This is especially true of colds and flu which are virus diseases. There really isn't a cure for them.

VACCINATION AGAINST DISEASE

An important way of reducing the risk of microbe diseases is *vaccination.* With some diseases your lymph cells build up a supply of antibodies which stay in the body long after the disease has gone. It also seems that the lymph cells 'remember' in some way and can quickly start to produce antibodies as soon as the same type of antigen enters the body as part of a microbe. This means that microbes are given no chance to multiply and so you do not suffer from the disease. We say that you are 'immune' to the disease.

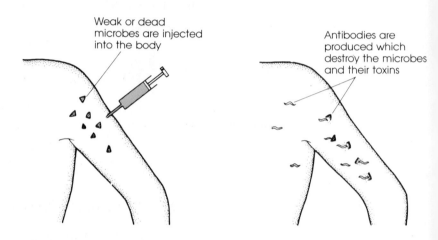

How vaccination works

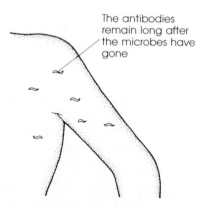

For some illnesses, like chickenpox, having the illness once is enough to build up the body's antibodies. The illness itself is quite mild and does not really need to be prevented. Other illnesses, like whooping cough, polio, diptheria and tuberculosis, can kill, and so we are vaccinated against them. Usually a liquid containing weak or dead microbes is injected into the body. For polio the liquid is taken by mouth and the microbes get into the blood through the gut wall.

Vaccinations work by giving you a very mild form of the disease. It is so mild that it does you no harm and you probably would not notice any effects at all. However, it is sufficient for the lymph cells to be able to build up antibodies against the disease. Many vaccinations require 'boosters' at some time to make sure that the antibody level remains high enough to keep us immune.

Table of Vaccinations

Diseases Vaccinated Against	Approximate Age
Diphtheria, Whooping cough, Tetanus (a triple vaccine)	6, 8 and 12 months
Diphtheria and Tetanus	5 years
Polio	6, 8, 12 months and 5 years
Measles	2 years
German measles	Girls only, 11–13 years
Tuberculosis	12–13 years

QUESTIONS ON INTERNAL DISEASES

For questions 1 and 2 fill in the missing words. Do not write on this page.

1   ____ and ____ are different sorts of microbes which may cause disease. These can be dealt with by the body's ____ ____ cells. There are two sorts of these cells, ____ and ____ cells.

2   The three stages of a microbe-caused disease are ____, ____ and ____.

3   Describe simply why microbes can make us ill and explain how the body deals with microbes.

4   Explain how vaccinations work.

5   List five diseases you have been vaccinated against and give your approximate age when you had each vaccination.

6   Measles is caused by a virus; which microbes cause the following diseases?

    tuberculosis, smallpox, whooping cough, tetanus, mumps, polio.

    For which of these diseases will the doctor give you antibiotics?

WORDFINDER ON MICROBES

Trace the wordfinder on to a piece of paper. Then solve the following clues and put a ring around the answers. Answers go in any direction: across, back, up, down and diagonally. The answer to Question 1 is ringed already to give you a start.

S	L	V	C	E	T	I	H	W	E
M	E	O	I	L	O	P	B	U	T
I	N	I	U	R	M	E	L	A	Y
C	O	L	D	Y	U	A	O	N	C
R	E	A	L	O	D	S	O	T	O
O	R	P	A	N	B	P	D	I	G
B	A	C	T	E	R	I	A	G	A
E	S	O	P	E	A	R	T	E	H
S	L	L	E	C	R	I	U	N	P
D	Y	T	O	X	I	N	C	S	A

1 Microbes may consume these as food (5)
2 Chemicals, made in the blood, which attack and destroy microbes (10)
3 Living organisms like these can reproduce every half-hour (8)
4 Organism which causes the cold (5)
5 3 and 4 are both types of these (8)
6 Poison produced by 5 (5)
7 Chemicals on 5 which cause the body to make 2 (8)
8 Often the only treatment a doctor may give for a cold is advice to take this (7)
9 Cells which make 2 (5)
10 A white blood cell which feeds on 3 (9)
11 A disease which you are vaccinated against at 6, 8 and 12 months and again at 5 years (5)
12 This contains different sorts of white cells (5)

CHAPTER 3
EXTERNAL DISEASES AND PARASITES

There are many disorders of the skin itself. Some are serious and need treatment by a doctor. Others can be successfully treated at home. All skin diseases are unpleasant, especially if they occur on the face or hands. We want other people to admire the way we look, and none of us feels our best if our skin looks blemished.

PSORIASIS

The skin, often around the knees or elbows, produces dull red spots which get larger and become bright red patches. They may often produce flaky, silvery-white scales characteristic of the condition. The cause of psoriasis is unknown and it must be treated by a doctor.

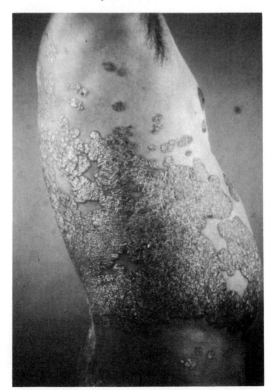

Psoriasis

SEBORRHOEA

This is the name given to the condition where there are lots of blackheads on the face and back. Its treatment is described more fully in Chapter 4.

WARTS

Warts are caused by viruses and are very easily caught from someone who has them. They are common on the hands but they can occur all over the body. They appear as dark round lumps, often in groups and after a length of time they seem to disappear. *Verrucas,* or plantar warts, are warts on the feet which have become flattened and are not raised above the surface of the skin. They are often painful and therefore need treatment.

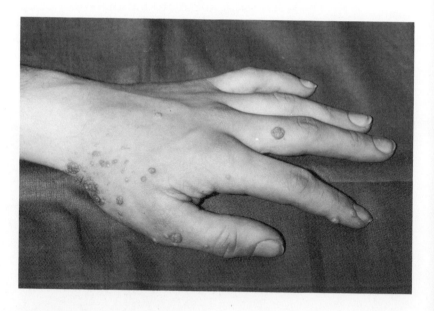

Warts

Warts can be removed by a doctor in various ways, all of which attempt to either cut away the infected skin or kill the virus by some means. This can take the dramatic form of using liquid nitrogen which is so cold it instantly kills the affected cells and stops the infection from spreading. Warts on the hands can be treated using special compounds available from a chemist.

RINGWORM

This disease is not caused by a worm at all but by a fungus. The fungus lives under the surface of the skin and spreads in a circle from the original centre of infection. This produces a circular patch of affected skin which gives the disease its name. The affected skin becomes scaley. Although it can occur on any part of the body it is common on the head. In this case the hair may be lost where the skin is infected. Ringworm is extremely contagious and must be treated by a doctor. Children with ringworm must stay away from school until the condition is cleared up. Treatment uses creams which quickly cure the infection.

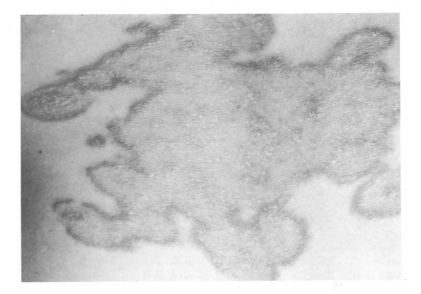

Ringworm

ATHLETE'S FOOT

This foot disease is caused by the same fungus as ringworm. It gets its name from the fact that it is usually picked up in

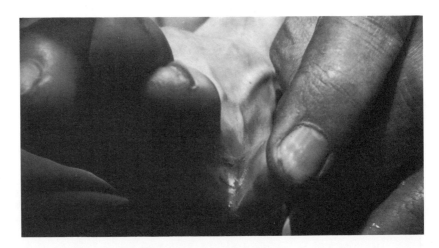

Athlete's foot

changing rooms, either at school or in public swimming baths. The disease is very contagious and affects the skin between the toes. It causes the skin to appear white and 'soaking wet'. Deep cracks appear in the skin. Treatment by a doctor is necessary, and while suffering from the disease a person should avoid passing it on at school. The games teacher should be informed and it may mean that games and PE are not possible until the disease has cleared up. (Note: the same may be true of verrucas.)

SKIN PARASITES

There are a number of animal parasites which live on the skin. Just the thought of having parasites makes our skin feel 'itchy' but, surprisingly, they are quite common. It is not only dirty people who suffer from them; they can just as easily transfer to a perfectly clean body. Once established, normal standards of cleanliness will not remove them — special treatments will be necessary.

Fleas

These parasites suck blood and being tall and thin, they can move easily through the fur of animals. They are not choosy about who their next meal comes from, and will frequently transfer from a cat or dog to people. The adults die within a few days if they cannot get food, so controlling them is not difficult. A good bath removes adult fleas from the body and any clothes which may be affected can be washed. Flea larvae can live in the dust and scraps found around the house, they do not suck blood. They thrive in centrally heated houses and, in consequence, fleas are becoming more of a problem. The pupa (the resting stage between larva and adult) can remain dormant for a long time and the adult will only emerge when disturbed by the

An adult flea

Seen from the front the flea is very narrow

Sucking mouthparts

Side view

Powerful jumping leg

nearness of a person or animal on which it can feed. It is possible to move into a house which has been empty for some months and to find fleas on you within a short space of time.

Lice

There are a number of different sorts of louse, the *head louse,* the *body louse* and the *pubic louse.* They are all very similar, being flattened insects which suck blood. Because they are flat they can grip on to the skin and are not easily dislodged. They all lay eggs called *nits* which are glued to the base of the hair. A female head louse can lay up to 60 eggs per month so infestations can quickly spread. The eggs hatch in about a week and take a further 2 weeks to become fully grown. Head lice are fairly common. You catch them usually by adult lice passing from person to person. This can happen when people get very close together or, in the case of head lice, when people share hats and combs. Because of this, it is usual to have inspections at school to check for nits.

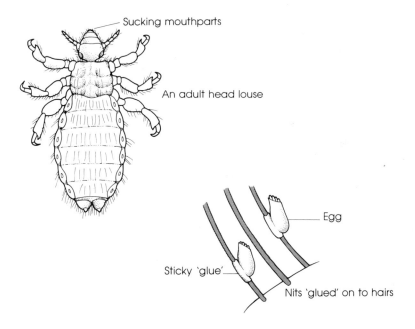

Head lice

You can, however, tell if you have head lice by the intense itching of your scalp. They can be treated by special insecticidal shampoos which are available from a chemist. Any eggs must be combed out of the hair using a comb with very small spaces between the teeth. These, too, are available from a chemist. A second shampoo about a week later will catch young lice which hatch from any eggs missed.

A comb to remove nits

Extremely narrow gaps between the teeth

Body lice and pubic lice (also known as 'crabs') are not as common as head lice. They are caught through close body contact, particularly in the case of pubic lice. It is possible that body lice can be caught in the same way as bedbugs, by sleeping on a bed after someone who was infected. Treatment is similar to that for head lice.

Mites

These are tiny blood-sucking animals related to spiders. *Scabies,* which is the medical name for the condition caused by mites, is quite common. The female makes a short tunnel under the skin and lays her eggs at the bottom of it.

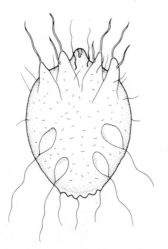

An adult mite

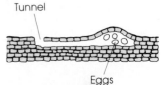

Tunnel

Eggs

The adult bores a tunnel in the horny layer of the skin and lays her eggs at the end of it

Tunnels are often found in the skin of the wrists and between the toes and fingers and are visible as thin wavy lines. The eggs hatch and the young mites crawl out on to the skin to feed. Scabies causes terrible itching which causes secondary infection because it is hard not to scratch. Scratching also spreads the infection. Treatment involves painting the skin with special lotions which must be left to penetrate the tunnels. All clothing must be carefully washed and treated with an insecticide.

Bedbugs

These are small animals which live in mattresses and crawl out at night to feed by sucking blood. They are very irritating, and scratching may allow other infections to start. They can live in tiny cracks in walls and even under the wallpaper. Your doctor and the local public health department will be able to help get rid of them.

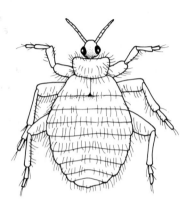

An adult bedbug

QUESTION ON PARASITES

Fill in the missing words. Do not write on this page.

Some skin parasites include ____ which may hop from dogs and cats to people. ____ are flattened insects which can grip on to the skin. They lay eggs called ____ which are stuck to the hairs. ____ are fairly common and are inspected for at school. ____ are parasites which are related to spiders. The condition they cause is called ____ .

CROSSWORD ON SKIN DISEASES AND PARASITES

First, trace this grid on to a piece of paper (or photocopy this page). Then fill in the answers. Do not write on this page.

Across

1. Ringworm is caused by a ___ (6)
4. A female mite will ___ her eggs at the end of a short tunnel (3)
5. We get 10 across on our ___ (4)
6. One of these is necessary to get rid of nits (5)
9. A skin disease, often found on the knees and elbows (9)
10. These sort of people often pick up a disease in changing rooms or swimming baths (8)
13. 1 down are animals which are tall and ___ (4)
14. See 9 down (5)
17. A flattened insect which sucks blood (5)

Down

1. Jumping insects which like the fur of animals (5)
2. An egg which is stuck to the base of a 11 down (3)
3. A bed bug ___ blood (5)
4. 14 across often appear as dark round ___ (5)
7. A disease caused by 8 down (7)
8. Tiny animals related to spiders (5)
9, 14 across Another name for verrucas (7, 5)
11. Something we have on our head (4)
12. 9 across often produces a characteristic silvery white ___ (5)
15. A structure you find on your foot (3)
16. Do doctors know what causes 9 across? (2)

CHAPTER 4

ACNE – A TEENAGE WORRY

SKIN

The state of our skin is often a very good indicator of how healthy the rest of our body is. Skin is a fairly tough, thin, elastic covering to the body and we have about 2 square metres of it. It is the largest organ of the body and has a number of jobs:

1) To hold the parts of the body together and to stop the body fluids from leaking away;
2) To protect the inner parts the body from invasion by microbes;
3) To make the body waterproof;
4) To help keep the body temperature at around 37°C by controlling the amount of heat loss;
5) To help to supply vitamin D to the body, which is made in the skin by the action of sunlight (vitamin D prevents the disease rickets);
6) To allow the body to be aware of its environment through the sense of touch, pain and temperature detection.

The skin also has special properties for maintaining itself:

1) It heals cuts and scratches;
2) It produces oil, called *sebum,* which keeps itself and the hair supple.

SKIN STRUCTURE

One estimate has suggested that one square centimetre of the skin contains about 3 million cells, 13 *sebaceous* (oil) glands, 100 sweat glands, 9 hairs, 3 metres of nerves, 1 metre of blood vessels and many hundreds of sensory cells.

In addition to this the outside layer of the skin is made of dead cells filled with a protein substance called *keratin.* These cells are constantly being rubbed off and on average they last for three or four weeks only. They are continuously replaced by living cells from below.

23

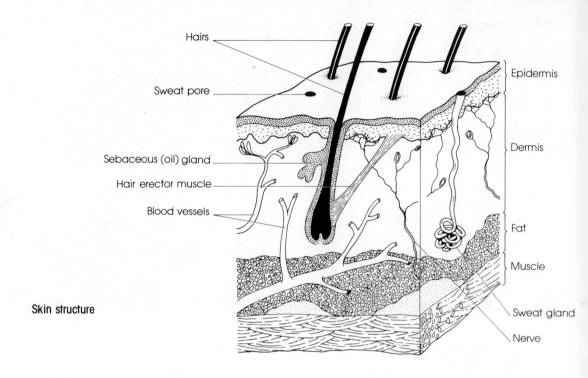

Skin structure

You can see that the skin is a very active and complicated organ which usually manages to work very well. Being so active it can easily get out of condition and needs to be looked after carefully. Illnesses in other parts of the body will often divert blood away from the skin, allowing its condition to deteriorate. A common first sign of illness is looking 'pale'.

ACNE

One of the commonest problems to affect a teenager's skin is acne or spots. The term 'acne' actually covers a whole range of conditions from a few blackheads on the chin to masses of large purple blotches covering the face, neck, shoulders and back. The very severe forms of acne occur in only 3 to 5 per cent of people and must be treated by a doctor. The mild forms of acne have been shown to occur in nearly everybody and usually during the teenage years. Spots are not a sign of uncleanliness or poor skin condition but these things can make them worse. One of the first things you should realise is that you may not be able to stop getting spots but you can prevent them from being a problem. You should also realise that after a year or two, for most people, the spots will stop of their own accord.

A common teenage problem

What is acne?

During puberty many changes take place in the body, changes which turn a young person's body into that of a man or woman. These changes are caused by chemical messengers called *hormones*, which are produced in quite large amounts at this time. There is an imbalance in the body's hormones and this often leads to acne.

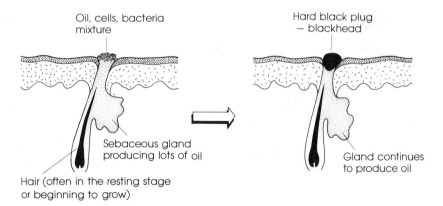

Formation of a blackhead

The sebaceous glands produce oil called *sebum*. This normally keeps the skin supple but when there is too much it tends to make the skin oily or greasy. The sebum tends to prevent the outside layers of skin from being shed and encourages the pores of the sebaceous glands to become blocked with sebum and hard skin cells. The glands meanwhile continue to produce sebum which cannot escape but stays in the entrance to the gland and mixes with dead skin cells and bacteria to form a hard plug. If the pore of the gland is large then the plug is exposed to the air. Chemical changes turn the plug to a black colour, resulting in a *blackhead* or *comedo*. Its colour is not caused by dirt but by the chemicals of the mixture. If the sebum remains under the skin because the pore is very small, then it does not become exposed to the air. It remains white and is called a *whitehead*.

Blackheads do not look very nice, but because the sebum mixture can leak away slowly they do not often turn into infected spots. Whiteheads are the major problem. Sebum builds up inside the passages of the gland; this build-up may become infected as the bacteria feed on the oil and cells. White blood cells move into the area to try to destroy the bacteria. Dead white cells and bacteria form the yellowy mixture known as *pus*. This then becomes the spot or pimple which we are all familiar with.

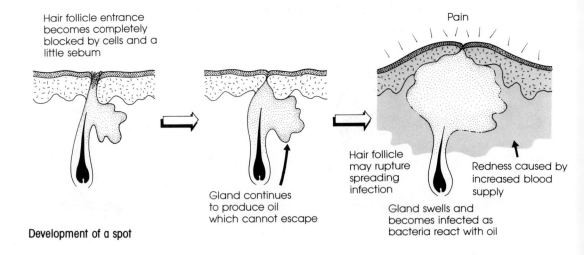

Development of a spot

In severe cases of acne the walls of the sebaceous gland break, spilling the contents into the surrounding tissues. This leads to a much larger spot which becomes swollen and reddish-purple as some more blood moves in to try to fight the infection. Squeezing and picking can also easily produce spots like this as the infected mixture is forced into the skin instead of out of it. This very large infected area is known as a *pustule*.

Controlling acne

You cannot stop acne, but you can limit its effects. The first and most important rule is to wash and wash again. A good wash in the morning is essential, and showering or bathing after physical exercise is also important. However, do remember that spots are not caused by being dirty so it is not necessary to scrub your skin. Washing with a mild soap or cleanser will help remove the oil and layer of cells and prevent the sebeceous glands from becoming blocked. If you scrub your skin or use soaps which have powerful grease-removing properties, then there is the risk that you will remove all the oil from the skin and dry it out. Dry skin may become red and cracked and look unsightly. You should try to wash gently using a soft flannel to work the soapy lather into the skin. Have your flannel regularly laundered by boiling; two clean flannels a week is a good idea. Rinse the lather off with warm water and then with cold to help close the pores. Dry the skin with a soft towel. If you suffer from blackheads, or only a very mild acne, then a brisk rub with the towel may help rub off dead skin cells and remove some of the blackheads. With severe acne, however, the rubbing is more likely to cause the spots to spread under the skin, so patting dry, rather than rubbing, is best.

Daily washing procedure

1) Wash with clean flannel

2) Rinse carefully with warm water, then cold

3) Dry with a soft towel (rub briskly for blackheads but only pat if you have severe acne)

Some soaps contain antiseptics which are claimed to destroy the bacteria which cause spots. This may be true if the antiseptic could reach the bacteria but in most acne the bacteria are deep in the sebaceous glands and way out of reach of most soaps. Such soaps may help a little with blackheads but do not be disappointed if they fail to limit your spots.

Although spots on the face often appear the most unsightly, spots also occur frequently on the neck and back. The same rules of washing apply here, too.

It used to be said that eating chocolate or lots of greasy foods made spots worse. Carefully controlled experiments have, however, been unable to show any proof of this, so restricting yourself to a severe diet will not make your spots go away and will probably stop you enjoying some of the foods you like. If, in your particular case, certain foods seem to increase your spots, then it would be sensible to avoid those foods, at least for a while. Remember, too, that no matter who you are or what your age is you should try to eat a balanced diet. This will allow your body to function as well as it can and will allow you to feel healthy. If you feel good, then your spots will not seem so bad.

The same is true of exercise and rest. Once again, it used to be said that plenty of exercise and lots of rest would help stop spots. This is not true, but as with a balanced diet the right combination of exercise and rest will make you feel better.

Emotional tension has been shown to affect acne. Spots may subside during the school holidays only to flare up again when term starts. Pre-menstrual tension in girls may make the problem worse just before a period. It may also flare up at exam time or if you have a job interview. There is little you can do about this except stick to the basic rules of cleanliness.

Don't pick your spots

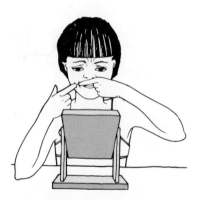

BE CAREFUL – you may do more harm than good

Picking spots can become a favourite occupation for some people. They seem to spend hours in front of a mirror pushing and squeezing each spot or blackhead. Probably everybody picks spots or blackheads at some time, but be warned — it can easily make the problem worse. Many doctors believe that some blackheads, if they are particularly unsightly, can be removed. A device called a *comedo extractor* is often recommended. If it is carefully used and cleaned after each use then it can be helpful. Occasionally fingernails may be used, provided great care is taken and a few simple rules are followed. Apart from cleaning the hands the same rules apply when using a comedo extractor:

1) First wash your hands and carefully scrub your fingernails.
2) Press some cotton wool which has been soaked in warm water on to the blackhead. This will help soften the skin and make removal easier.
3) Gently squeeze the area to remove the blackhead entirely.
4) Dab the area with a little antiseptic.
5) Wash your hands and the comedo extractor.

Spots, especially the large purplish blotches, should never be picked. There is too great a risk that the pus will be squeezed out through the side of the sebaceous gland and further into the skin. This just increases the area infected and does no good at all. The after-effects of picking spots may, in the end, be much worse than the spots themselves. Wounds caused by nails slipping or cutting the skin will heal by production of small amounts of scar tissue. This leaves the skin permanently scarred and unsightly, especially on the face. You would be foolish to jeopardise your future looks in order to get some temporary relief.

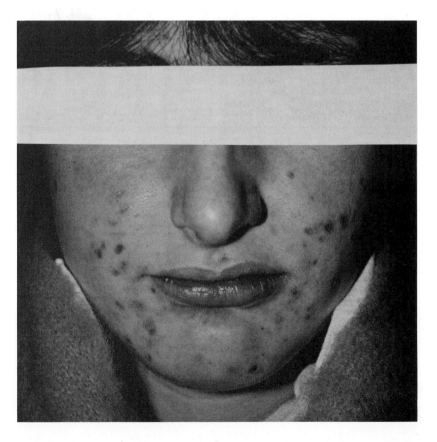

This condition needs medical treatment

There are many creams and lotions available from a chemist for use on acne. They are unlikely to have much effect on many of your spots because spots begin so deep in the skin. The creams are not able to penetrate far into the skin and therefore cannot really attack the infection. Substances which can penetrate the skin are a little more difficult to use properly and so are available only through your doctor who will give you precise instructions on their use. The acne creams you can buy will have some effect on blackheads and a few of your spots. They work by peeling away the blackheads and therefore unblocking the pores. The active ingredients of such compounds are either resorcinol, salicylic acid or occasionally benzoyl peroxide, or some combination of these. You may have some success with them on your blackheads but do not expect them to work miracles on more severe acne. Perhaps some of the best ones to use are those which are flesh-coloured, because at least they hide the spots a little. You can, of course, use a little non-greasy make-up to hide your spots, too, provided it is thoroughly removed each night.

Some occupations are known to encourage acne. Engineers who work with machine oils a lot are liable to suffer from acne because the oils block up the pores. This can often happen where clothes become oil-soaked and are in constant contact with the skin. Students who spend lessons with their chin cupped in their hands for support can also make acne worse because this encourages blocked pores. Young people, too, who work in hamburger restaurants or similar eating places have been shown to be more prone to acne because of the contact with cooking oils and fats. In America, where this condition was first identified, it has been called 'McDonald's Acne'. People with these sorts of occupation must take extra care with daily washing.

Acne — the rules

The simple rules for the treatment of acne are:

1) Wash at least twice a day, more if possible.
2) Do not pick your spots.
3) Try not to worry about acne, it will not help and could make it worse.
4) A balanced diet, exercise and rest will make you feel better and by feeling better you can more easily live with your spots.

ACTIVITY 3

Experiment to investigate the grease-removing properties of soaps

1) Take four clean glass slides and four clean petri dishes. Label one of each A, B, C and D.

2) Make up four different soap solutions as follows: Dissolve 0.1 g of any household soap in 100 cm^3 of water. Warming the water will help dissolve the soap but cool the solution down to room temperature for the experiment. Since you will only need 20 to 25 cm^3 of each soap solution you can work in groups to prepare four different solutions.

3) Pour a different soap solution into each petri dish.

4) Paint one side of each glass slide with a thin, even layer of olive oil which has been stained with alcoholic eosin stain (or something similar).

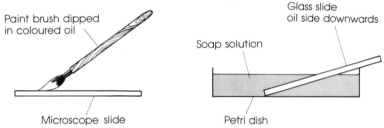

5) Start the stop-clock and quickly put the slides, oil side down, into the petri dishes. Rest the slide on the edge of the dish as in the diagram. Remember, slide A goes in dish A, etc.

6) After 5 minutes remove the slides and lay them oil side up on a paper towel. Compare the slides to see which soap solution has removed the most oil.

7) Replace the slides in the petri dishes for a further 5 minutes. Remove them and again compare to see which soap solution is most effective at dissolving the oil.

8) If there is time, continue the experiment until one solution dissolves away all the olive oil.

9) The experiment can be repeated with other soap solutions.

ACTIVITY 4

Adverts

Many treatments for spots are advertised on TV and in magazines. Collect a few of these adverts and assess them. Try to decide whether the claims are scientific. Do the products have a 'miracle' ingredient? How good is this proof? Can you design an experiment to test how good the product is?

ACTIVITY 5

Problem page

'Lonely' of Oxington has written to the problem page of a teenage magazine. She says that she has greasy skin and acne and feels so awful that she rarely goes out. Sometimes her friend persuades her to go to a disco, but she always sits in the darkest corner because she is afraid that the boys will laugh at her or think her ugly. What advice would you offer?

ACTIVITY 6

A shy friend

Pete is your friend. He is good at sport, playing football and cricket, and swimming. He has a good physique but suffers badly from acne. Pete is rather shy at the best of times, but you know him to be a sincere person. You also know that several girls would like to go out with him, but his shyness and his awareness of his acne mean that he would never ask them out. How would you convince Pete that his acne is not really a problem and that girls will not laugh at him?

QUESTIONS ON SKIN

Fill in the missing words for questions 1, 2 and 3. Do not write on this page.

1. Your skin has several jobs. It ____ the body together and ____ the body from invasion by ____ of some sort. It makes the body ____ and helps control body ____ by controlling the amount of ____ lost. It also makes ____ ____ by the action of sunlight.

2. Spots is a common name for ____. Many teenagers suffer from this because of changes caused by ____ which are often out of balance during ____.

3. Spots are caused by a mixture of ____ produced by the sebaceous glands, dead ____ cells and ____. If exposed to the air the mixture will turn ____ in colour, which produces a ____.

4. To keep your skin and body healthy, you need a balanced diet. Explain what this means.

5. Draw a diagram or diagrams to show how a spot forms. Write down in your own words what you can do to help control spots.

CROSSWORD ON SKIN

First, trace this grid on to a piece of paper (or photocopy this page). Then fill in the answers. Do not write on this page.

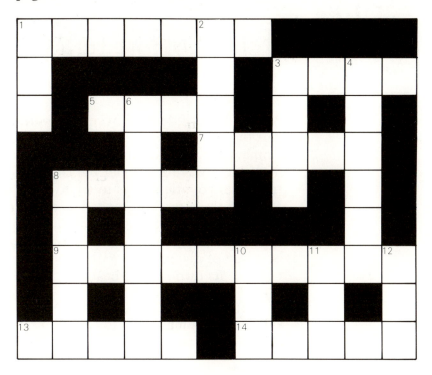

Across

1. 5 across contains many hundreds of ___ cells (7)
3. Where you can't see the acne? (4)
5. Our largest organ (4)
7. Oil from 5 across (5)
8. How many metres of nerves are there in a square centimetre of 5 across? (5)
9. 5 across keeps the body ___ (10)
13. See 14 across
14, 13 across   It opens on to the 5 across (5, 5)

Down

1. It helps produce vitamin D (3)
2. After washing you should ___ your face carefully with warm water (5)
3. My skin may be very soft! (4)
4. Another name for a blackhead (6)
6. The protein in dead 5 across cells (7)
8. A dirty one won't help acne (5)
10. A yellowy mixture that can form a spot (3)
11. How many metres of blood vessels are there in a square centimetre of 5 across (3)
12. Cooking ___ won't help acne (3)

STANLEY COMPREHENSIVE SCHOOL,
TYNE ROAD,
STANLEY,
CO. DURHAM.

CHAPTER 5
HAIR – A GROWING PROBLEM

Although hair grows all over our bodies, it is really only the hair on our heads that concerns us here. The Egyptians and Romans had ways of improving the look of their hair by dyeing and waving it. Over the centuries hair has been treated in countless ways to try to make it look better. Many of these methods ended by making the hair much worse. The treatments were so harsh that they made the hair fall out or go dry or produced alarming dandruff. The best way of making hair look good is by working with it to enhance its own natural beauty.

WHAT IS HAIR?

Hair is a series of protein tubes. There are three tubes inside one another. The inner one is the *medulla* which is quite spongy. It contains air spaces and so affects the sheen and

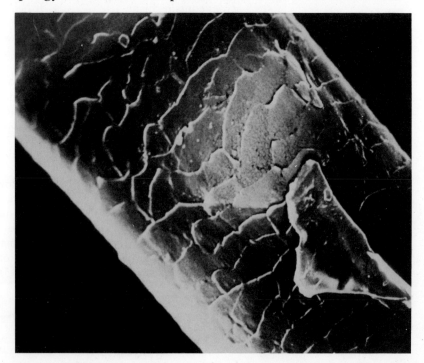

A hair under a microscope

34

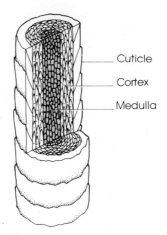

A hair cut open to show its structure

colour of the hair by affecting how light is reflected. The middle tube is the *cortex* which contains the substances which give the hair its colour. The outside layer is the *cuticle* and it is made of tiny transparent scales which overlap each other. The cuticle keeps the cortex together and stops it from fraying.

HAIR GROWTH

The hair grows from a small pit in the skin called a *follicle*. In the bottom of the follicle is a group of cells called the *papilla*, which actually make the hair. The hair grows, therefore, from the base and the tip is the oldest part. This is why, after having hair bleached or dyed, the original colour reappears nearest the scalp when the new hair, which was not dyed, is pushed up.

Hair grows in a cycle. Each hair has a growing stage, a stage where the hair stops growing and changes into a club hair,

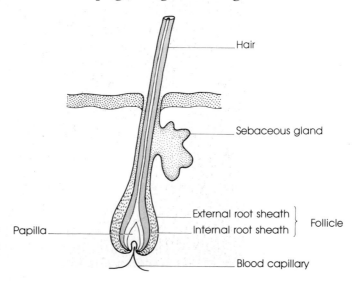

A section through a hair follicle

and a resting stage. A club hair has a swollen base which is anchored only a little way into the skin. After the resting stage a new hair begins to grow in the follicle of the club hair. The old hair falls out sometime during the resting stage.

The length of a person's hair is determined by the length of the growing stage and the speed with which the hair grows. This is different for different people and explains why some people can grow very long hair while others cannot.

Factors affecting hair growth

On average, hair grows between 0.5 and 1 cm per month. This can vary with different conditions. For example, hair grows faster in the summer than the winter. Growth is fastest between the ages of 15 and 30 years. Hormone changes can affect growth too, especially in older people. In men, growth may stop, leading to baldness. In women, unwanted facial hair may result from hormone changes. Cutting hair, however, does not affect the rate at which hair grows. It may appear that you have more hair or that it is growing more quickly but this is simply the result of the way it is cut. It is said that a hair pulled out of your scalp will take 5 to 6 months to be replaced. This is a good reason for taking care of your hair.

A hair may last for between 6 months and 6 years, but an average lifespan is 2 to 4 years. We lose about 30 hairs per day but this can be increased by careless combing or brushing or harsh hair treatments.

HAIR CARE

The best way to keep hair healthy is to keep it clean. A good shampoo should be used and you should remember that the gentle massaging of the scalp is as important as getting a good lather. You should work over the entire scalp to stimulate the blood vessels and remove dead skin.

Carefully rinse off the shampoo using clean water. Rinse your hair until it 'squeaks'. This will tell you that all the shampoo has been removed. It is impossible to over-rinse your hair. You should use warm water, not too hot or too cold, and you should work the water through the hair. If you us a jug or shower, then get the water as close as possible to the head; otherwise the water will simply bounce off the hair and not penetrate it. It is no good rinsing your hair in the bath water; clean water is essential.

When drying your hair pat it dry with a towel, but do not rub it too hard because this could lead to hair breaking. When using a hair dryer avoid using very hot air. This tends to affect the natural oils of the scalp and can make the hair brittle.

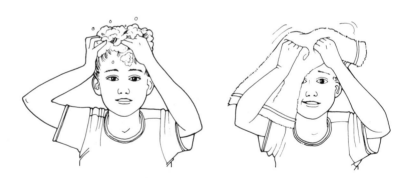

Regular brushing helps keep the hair in good condition because it helps to remove dirt and grime and stimulates the blood to flow to the skin. Use a brush which is not too soft since this will merely smooth down the hair. It is important for the bristles to penetrate between the hairs and reach down to the scalp.

Remember, too, that brushes and combs can harbour dirt and they should be cleaned each week. A little disinfectant in the water will help control possible infection. Do not share combs or brushes because this can lead to diseases (e.g. head lice) being passed between people.

Wash combs and brushes often

It is possible to buy shampoos specifically for dry hair, greasy or fine hair. As a rule, though, greasy hair needs washing about once every three to four days, dry hair once a week and brittle or damaged hair every ten days. For dry or damaged hair a conditioner is advisable.

DANDRUFF

Almost everybody suffers from dandruff at some stage of their life. It is a nuisance and may be an embarrassment, but more than this it is a minor disease. Dandruff is dead skin from the head which flakes off and becomes entangled in the hair. The shedding of dead skin cells is quite normal but dandruff occurs when the cells get mixed up with sebum to form scaley particles. Dandruff coincides with too much oil being produced by the sebaceous glands and often accompanies acne as a teenage problem.

Dandruff

There is not really a cure for dandruff but, as with other skin conditions, it can be limited. It seems, too, that leading a highly stressed life may encourage dandruff.

The best treatment is to use a shampoo which removes the oil and skin mixture and so limits the build-up of scales. Shampoos for greasy hair will not do this; special shampoos are necessary. These often contain the active ingredient *selenium sulphide* which should be used with care. The hair must be thoroughly rinsed after washing, and care must be taken to avoid getting any shampoo in the eyes. Selenium sulphide also discolours jewellery, so rings should be removed before using it. These shampoos should not be used each time the hair is washed but should be used regularly. Another common ingredient of shampoos for dandruff control is *zinc pyrithione*. This has been proven to be effective against dandruff and is not quite as harmful as selenium sulphide. Whichever ingredient your shampoo contains it is important to allow it a couple of minutes to work on your hair. Carefully follow the manufacturer's instructions. Other 'medicated' shampoos usually only contain an antiseptic which may or may not have any real affect on dandruff.

If dandruff is not treated, then it can lead to other minor diseases because the scaly layer makes an ideal place for microbes to grow. If you have serious dandruff and are worried about it because ordinary treatment is not making it better, then you should consult your doctor.

ACTIVITY 7

Experiment to test the abilities of different shampoos to remove grease

Repeat activity 3 on page 31 but this time use a solution of shampoos instead of soaps. Make up the shampoo solutions by putting one drop of shampoo into 25 cm^3 of water.

ACTIVITY 8

An investigation into dandruff shampoos

Make a list of dandruff shampoos and find out what active ingredient each one contains. Which ones contain only an antiseptic? Do a survey among your class or friends to find out which dandruff shampoos seem to work best.

ACTIVITY 9

Perming and dyeing

Mandy arrives at school with purple hair which she has had permed perfectly straight. She says that when she gets tired of the colour and style she will change it. The colour can be removed with Subtractone and she can have another perm.

Gina thinks this is a fun idea, but Louise thinks it may not be good for Mandy's hair. What do you think? Explain your opinion.

You may already know enough to discuss the problem but if you do not, then you will have to research what colouring and perming can do to your hair.

QUESTIONS ON HAIR

Fill in the missing words in questions 1, 2 and 3. Do not write on this page.

1 Hair is a series of three tubes made of ____ . The inner tube is called the ____ , the middle is called the ____ and the outer tube is the ____ .
Draw a simple sketch to show how a hair is constructed.

2 Hair grows in a pit called a ____ . The growing region is called the ____ . The oldest part of the hair is the ____ .

3 Hairs grow at between ____ and ____ cm per month. Hairs grow faster in the ____ than in the ____ and people between the ages of ____ and ____ will grow their hair more quickly than other people.

4 Hair washing is very important. Describe how it should be done.

5 Write down all the things *you* do to look after your skin and hair. Then write down the things you do not do but think you ought to.

CROSSWORD ON HAIR

First, trace this grid on to a piece of paper (or photocopy this page. Then fill in the answers. Do not write on this page.

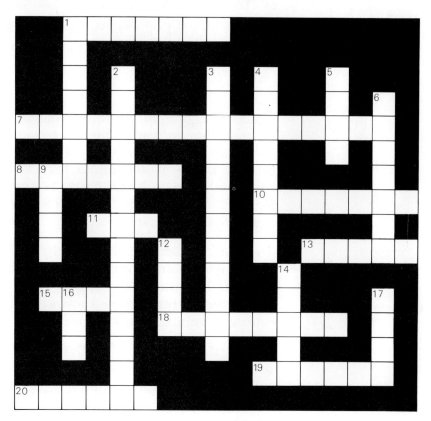

Across

1. 5 down is made of this (7)
7. Substance used to treat 16 across which discolours jewellery (8, 8)
8. Used to clean 5 down (7)
10. Part of 5 down, made of tiny scales (7)
11. ___ 5 down needs washing once a week (3)
13. Always rinse your 5 down with ___ water (5)
15. Use 8 across to ___ 5 down (4)
18. A minor disease of the scalp (8)
19. On average we lose this number of hairs per day (6)
20. Gives 5 down its colour (6)

Down

1. Where 5 down is made (7)
2. An ingredient used to treat 16 across. Not as harmful as 7 across (4, 10)
3. Clean your combs and brushes with this (12)
4. Small pit where 5 down grows (8)
5. It grows on your 9 down (4)
6. Middle part of a hair (7)
9. The ___ teacher runs your school (4)
12. Older men sometimes become this (4)
14. Do not use a ___ which is too soft (5)
16. 6 down has spaces filled with this (3)
17. A person's hair may start to look ___ as he gets older (4)

41

CHAPTER 6
CANCER – A MAJOR MALFUNCTION

Cancer is a common and often frightening disease. In fact it is not a single disease: there are over 200 forms of cancer. There are also many substances that we know of, which will cause it. Cancer is so complex that the only thing we can be completely sure of is that we do not really understand it. Research is going on all over the world into what cancer is and how to detect and treat it.

The word 'cancer' was first used by doctors who noticed that some abnormal cells grew and multiplied and spread through the surrounding tissues. These cells spread out to give shapes rather like the claws of a crab. Hence the name cancer, from the Latin word for crab.

Cancer, then, is an abnormal growth in the body where some cells start to grow and multiply and spread. Cancer cells are abnormal in that they do not do anything for the body. They just grow and multiply and use up food and oxygen that normal body cells could have used. Eventually these cells may squeeze normal cells out of the way and take over parts of an organ. If a large enough part is taken over then the body can no longer work and it dies.

There are some words, associated with cancer, which need sorting out. Cancer cells often grow into a lump; this lump is called a *tumour*. Cancer tumours are described as *malignant* because the cells spread out from the tumour to other tissues. Cells may also break off a malignant tumour and spread through the lymphatic system and bloodstream to other parts of the body. Wherever they end up they continue to grow and multiply to produce new malignant tumours. In this way cancer may spread throughout the body.

There are other sorts of tumours which are not cancer. These are called *benign tumours*. They are balls of abnormal cells which again just grow and multiply. The important feature of these cells is that they cannot spread through surrounding tissue. This means that if necessary a benign tumour can be completely removed by surgery, leaving no trace. The untreated ball or lump may get bigger and squeeze normal cells around it, but this does not always lead to serious harm.

There are, of course, lumps in the body which are not tumours. Sometimes too many normal cells grow, producing a lump which is completely harmless. Fat is often deposited in small lumps or we may get liquid-filled cysts. Warts, too, are lumps but they are certainly not cancer.

Cancer cells, therefore, are abnormal; they do nothing for the body at all. They just grow, multiply and spread. Cancer is such a complex disease and, as you have read, there are many different sorts. Therefore it is impossible to say how quickly the disease will spread. Even with the same type of cancer, in one person it can spread throughout the body in only a few months. In another person it can take many years.

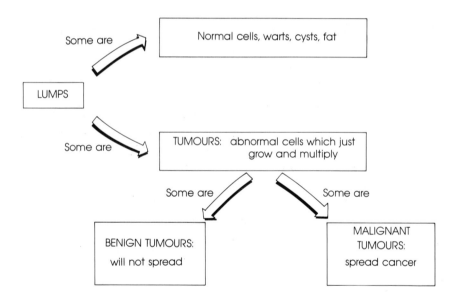

Why cells should suddenly grow into cancer cells no one is yet able to answer. It is thought that cancer is started by several factors all working together. Some substances seem to be able to change the way in which a cell works. These substances are called carcinogens. It seems that some carcinogens trigger the growth of cancer cells. Others do not actually start cancer but make it easier for the trigger carcinogens to work.

The complex way in which all these factors work together may explain why some people develop cancer but others in similar circumstances do not.

The number of known carcinogens is rising all the time as more research is done. Tobacco smoke is known to contain quite a few of them, which is why people who smoke are much more likely to develop lung cancer. Even sunlight can be a carcinogen — fair-skinned people who sunbathe a great deal are more likely to develop skin cancer as they get older than people who do not, although this form of cancer is not common in the United Kingdom.

The damage caused by cancer is not caused by poisons. Tumours push normal, healthy cells out of the way and use up their food supply. In an organ like the lungs, normal lung tissue is replaced by tumours. There may be bleeding around tumours which allows infections to enter. Gradually the lung is less and less able to do its job of getting oxygen into the blood. Death is the end result, although it is not usually caused simply by lack of lung tissue. Complications and secondary infections weaken the body until it is no longer able to sustain life. This process of dying can take years, or in some cases only a few weeks or months.

Lymphocytes are present in the blood to help fight infection. Normal lymphocytes are spherical in shape, but in the cancer known as hairy cell leukaemia, spikes and flaps develop on the cell, giving it a hairy appearance

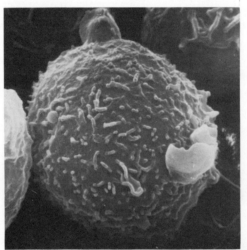

Normal cell

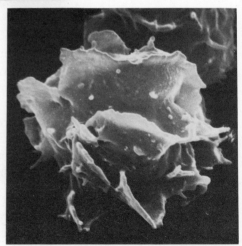

Hairy cell

FORMS OF TREATMENT

There are several different treatments for cancer, but in general they all try to remove or kill cancer cells. Early treatments include cutting out the tumour. This is still one of the most effective ways of treating cancer if the tumour is discovered early enough. Because of the problem of malignant tumours spreading, the surgeon may have to remove a lot of tissue around the tumour itself. Drugs and X-rays may be used after an operation like this to kill any cancer cells which may be left in the body.

X-rays or drugs can be used on their own to kill cancer cells. X-rays always kill some normal cells (which is why pregnant women are no longer X-rayed to see how the baby is developing). Normally the number of cells damaged is not very significant. A dense beam of X-rays can be used to deliberately kill and destroy cells. The beam can be aimed at the tumour and will destroy it. The problem is of course that healthy cells are destroyed at the same time. X-rays can only be used where the tumour's position is accurately known and where other healthy organs are not in the way. Also, not all tumours are affected by X-rays. Drugs can be used which are taken up by growing cells. This form of treatment is known as *chemotherapy*. These drugs kill the cell as it grows. Unfortunately the body is full of growing cells and these, too, are killed. The drug cannot choose only the cancer cells. Such treatment is severe and a common

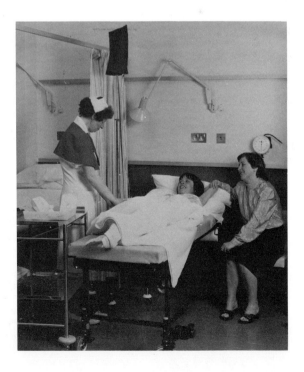

A young patient receiving chemotherapy, a form of treatment that is proving very successful for certain types of cancer

side-effect is that the patient loses all their hair. The treatment can for a while seem worse than the cancer itself. The body has, however, enormous powers of recovery and can restore itself to full health and with luck all the cancer will have been destroyed. Much of the research being done at the moment is on finding drugs which are effective against cancer but more gentle in their action. With early enough treatment not all cancers lead to death. For example, the treatment of leukaemia in children is now usually successful. Women who develop breast cancer have an excellent chance of being successfully treated. Similarly cancer of the testes in men is often curable. In general, the deeper inside the body the cancer is then the more problems it causes, usually because deep tumours are more difficult to find.

Before cancer can be treated it must be identified. A tumour near the surface of the body can sometimes be felt as a hard lump. Cancers inside the body need to be discovered using modern technology. X-rays will show up tumours and increasingly nowadays use is made of *X-ray scanners*. These can be used to scan the whole body and will produce a two-dimensional picture on a television screen. Tumours can show up as dark patches and their exact position inside the body can be seen. The illustration shows a scanner being used.

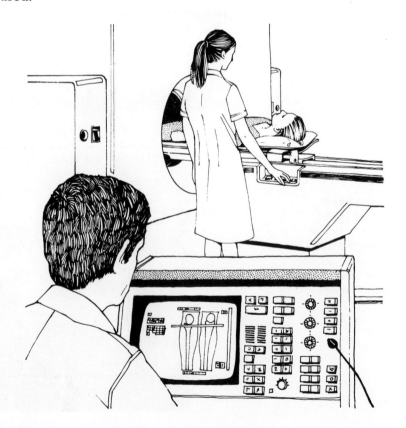

A body scanner can detect tumours

What can you do about cancer? 40,000 people die each year from lung cancer. Since almost all lung cancers are caused by smoking, you can avoid a lot of risk by not starting to smoke. Avoiding other known carcinogens is also an obvious course of action. Other than this you can do little. You can routinely check you body for signs of unusual lumps. This is particularly advisable for women, who can easily examine their breasts for any abnormal lumps — a leaflet on self-examination should be available from the doctor. Remember too, that most breast tumours are benign and therefore not so dangerous. *Cancers rarely occur in teenagers so you do not need to start worrying.* In older people, say 25 years or more, unusual symptoms such as odd pains should be checked with the doctor, if there is not an obvious cause. As with most diseases, the earlier the diagnosis then the more effective the treatment can be.

QUESTIONS ON CANCER

1 Explain what cancer is. What sorts of treatments are available for cancer?

2 What is a scanner? What does it do?

WORDFINDER ON CANCER

Hidden in this wordfinder is a ten-word message (length of words: 6, 10, 6, 7, 10, 3, 9, 6, 4, 6) offering advice on how to avoid lung cancer. Copy out the grid to find the words, then write the message underneath. Do not write on this page.

G	H	E	A	L	T	H	E	D	I
F	O	T	E	M	P	G	C	A	N
T	E	V	H	D	A	S	A	N	Y
N	O	W	E	M	H	E	N	G	O
C	I	G	A	R	E	T	T	E	S
F	F	D	L	E	N	R	E	R	D
R	G	F	T	A	G	M	E	U	O
U	N	A	H	O	U	S	E	I	O
O	U	T	W	A	R	N	I	N	G
Y	L	S	U	O	I	R	E	S	T

47

CHAPTER 7

WHEN PARTS FAIL

Problems are obviously caused when parts of the body stop working or begin to work less efficiently. Normally your body is well enough constructed to last for seventy or more years, but in some cases certain parts stop working before that time. Sometimes this is fatal, but in other cases it is possible to repair, replace or substitute the broken part. You will have heard of heart and kidney transplants — modern feats of medicine which, although no longer rare, are still extraordinarily complex operations. Replacement is only one way of dealing with problems. Doctors also try to repair damaged organs or find some way of substituting for them in the body. The following sections will show you some of the things which could go wrong and what can be done about them.

HEART DISEASES

The heart is a complex organ whose job is to pump blood around the body. Blood is vitally important, especially for the oxygen it carries from the lungs to the rest of the body. In fact your brain can survive for only about 4 minutes without oxygen. If your heart stops pumping, then there is not much time to get it going again.

Why should the heart stop working? The most common reason is that it runs out of oxygen. The muscle of the heart gets its oxygenated blood through the coronary artery and its branches (see diagram (a) opposite). This artery or its branches may become blocked and so the oxygen supply to the heart is stopped. The heart muscle then stops working. This is called a *heart attack*. It often occurs quite suddenly and is the biggest single killer in the United Kingdom.

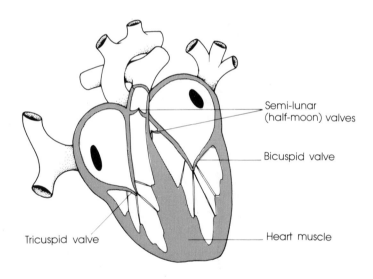

(a) The heart seen from the front

(b) The heart cut open

There are a number of factors which could lead to a heart attack:

1) Too much *cholesterol* — a fatty substance found in all meat. When there is too much in the blood it becomes deposited on the wall of arteries. This makes the central tube narrower. The coronary arteries have an enormous blood supply so the chances are that deposits will occur here. A deposit may break off and pass down the artery until it jams in the small artery, blocking it completely.

How arteries can become blocked by fat

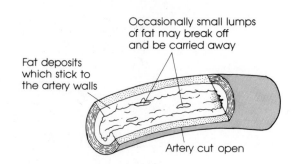

2) High blood pressure, making the heart work harder to force the blood around the body. The harder the heart must work, the more oxygen it needs and the greater the risk that this oxygen supply may fail.
3) Worry, which may lead to high blood pressure especially in conjunction with any of the other causes of heart attacks.
4) *Obesity*, which is being overweight, having too much fat. Obesity may lead to cholesterol deposits in arteries and certainly leads to higher blood pressure.
5) Smoking and drinking, which usually go with a lack of physical fitness. Smoking actually increases blood pressure. Drinking may lead to weight problems.

Most people who have heart attacks have some combination of the above factors.

Twenty years of not really looking after your body can, and often does, lead to a heart attack. The only way to be sure of avoiding this is to avoid as many of the causes as possible.

Apart from heart attacks, the heart itself may become diseased. In this case it may be possible to replace the heart with one from another person. This is a tricky operation, as the next Activity will show.

ACTIVITY 10

Surgical problems

1) Look at diagram (a) on page 49. Count the number of blood vessels which have to be cut and rejoined. Estimate how long it might take to join two blood vessels together.
2) Try to find out what happens to the patient's blood during a heart transplant.
3) Look at your own body. How many parts will the surgeon have to cut through to get to the heart? What problems does this create?

Another problem with heart transplants is *rejection*. The patient's body recognises that the new heart is in some way different and so treats it just like an invasion of microbes. The cells of the patient's blood vessels do not join with the heart cells and the transplant does not work. To help prevent rejection, the patient is given drugs which stop the body from recognising 'foreign' organisms. This of course means that the body doesn't recognise microbes either, which may lead to infections starting. For this reason, transplant patients must be kept in very hygienic conditions.

The transplanted heart must come from a donor who is dead. We know that the heart will continue to beat for several hours if it is kept warm and supplied with food and oxygen. A heart can be preserved alive in ice for longer. If the heart is still beating, how would you decide that the donor was dead? This is a question for discussion.

The heart has valves (see diagram (b) on page 49) which make sure the blood flows in one direction only. These valves are thin flaps of tissue which can break. This allows the blood to flow backwards in the heart. Damaged valves can be replaced by surgery.

The heart's beating is controlled by a patch of special muscle at the top of the right atrium. Sometimes this patch, called the pacemaker, stops working efficiently and the heart slows down. A tiny electrical device can be implanted to take the place of this pacemaker. This, too, is called a *pacemaker* and it sends tiny electric shocks into the heart at regular intervals to make it beat. The pacemaker is fitted within the muscle of the chest. A wire from it is inserted into a nearby vein, often the subclavian vein. The wire, with its electrode tip, is pushed down the vein and into the anterior vena cava which goes to the heart. The wire, therefore, has a clear passage

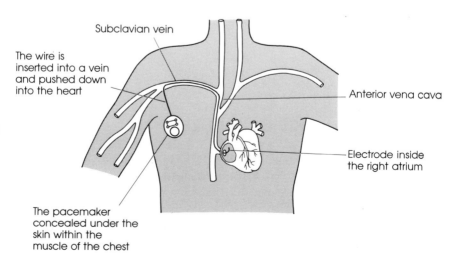

How a pacemaker is fitted

into the right atrium. It is pushed into the muscle wall at the top. The pacemaker is powered by batteries which nowadays last for up to 10 years. Also available, but still too expensive to be widely used, is a nuclear-powered battery which will last for more than 80 years.

ACTIVITY 11

The heart

1) Obtain a fresh, entire lamb's or pig's heart from a slaughter-house or butcher. If possible, get one with the lungs still attached.
2) Observe the arteries and veins which enter and leave the heart.
3) Carefully cut open the heart as shown in the diagram. This will allow you to see the tricuspid valve (cut 1), the semi-lunar valves of the pulmonary artery (cut 2), the bicuspid valve from above, showing how it shuts off the blood flow (cut 3), and the bicuspid valve from the side (cut 4).
4) Compare the thickness of the right and left ventricle walls. Explain why the left ventricle wall is so much thicker than that of the right.

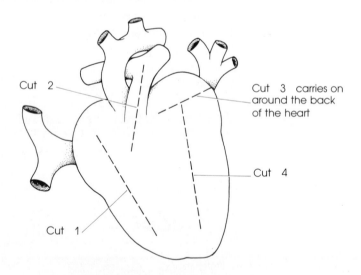

How to cut open a heart

KIDNEY FAILURE

Your two kidneys remove waste products produced by your body. These are dumped by the various parts of the body into the blood. The kidneys filter them out of the blood. In addition the kidneys make sure that the water level of the body remains constant by getting rid of excess water. The liquid produced, a mixture of water and wastes, is called

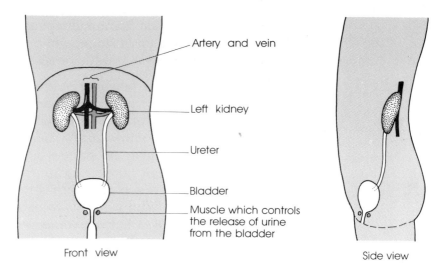

The position of the kidneys in the body

Front view   Side view

urine. It is stored in the bladder and, at convenient intervals, removed.

A kidney failure means that the waste products build up. Since some of them are poisonous they will quite quickly kill. Either the wastes must be removed artificially by a *kidney machine* or a new kidney must be transplanted in. You should remember, though, that although you have two kidneys, you can survive easily with one. Drastic measures are only necessary when both kidneys fail.

Patients on a kidney machine, or *dialysis machine,* must regularly spend hours attached to the machine. The blood is drawn out of a vein, passed through the machine, where it is cleaned, and then passed back again. The process can be slow and the machines are expensive. Many patients have to go to hospital twice a week for treatment. A number of

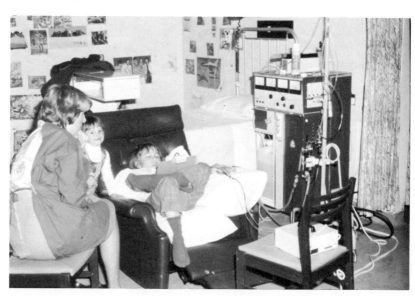

A patient on a dialysis machine

53

charities try to provide home kidney machines so that a patient can have dialysis at night while they are asleep and this disrupts their life as little as possible.

Kidney transplants are nowhere near as complex as heart transplants. The major problem is finding enough suitable donors. The majority of donors are dead road accident victims and many people now carry a kidney donor card. This allows doctors to remove the kidneys before they deteriorate, without having to wait for permission from the next-of-kin. The new donor cards also give permission for eyes, heart, liver, pituitary gland and pancreas to be removed, all of which may be useful in helping someone else to live.

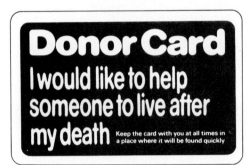 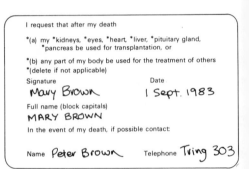

DIABETES

Diabetes is due to a failure of the pancreas. This organ, which lies just below the stomach, has two jobs. One is to produce enzymes to digest food in the duodenum and small intestine. The other is to produce the hormone *insulin* which helps to control the blood sugar level.

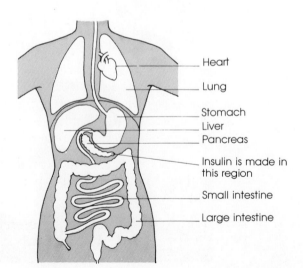

The position of the pancreas

After a meal, large amounts of glucose pass into the blood from the gut. This glucose is not all needed at once and if it stayed in the blood it would be filtered out by the kidneys. To prevent this, the liver converts glucose to a substance which can be stored, called *glycogen*. The presence of insulin makes the liver do this. Gradually, as the glucose is used by the body the liver turns glycogen back into glucose. This happens because the levels of insulin fall too.

Diabetes occurs when the pancreas fails to produce insulin. There are two sorts of diabetes. In one the pancreas stops making insulin altogether. This is called 'juvenile' diabetes because it occurs in younger people up to about twenty-five years of age. Older people can develop the 'adult' diabetes where the pancreas produces less insulin than is necessary.

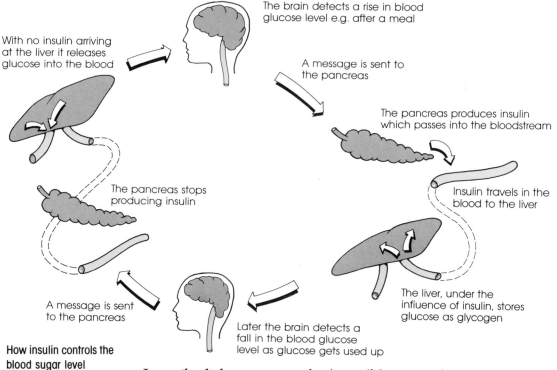

How insulin controls the blood sugar level

Juvenile diabetes cannot be 'cured' because the pancreas cannot be made to work again, but the insulin can be substituted. Daily injections of insulin will make the liver store glycogen. As the insulin is broken down and removed during the day then the liver releases glucose.

Adult diabetes can be treated with drugs which increase the amount of insulin that is produced. Insulin injections may not then be necessary.

Treatment for both types of diabetes must also include a diet of regular small meals to supply a steady flow of glucose It is important that diabetics balance the amount of insulin with the amount of glucose that they eat. Too little or too much glucose can lead to the person going into a coma possibly followed by death if treatment is not applied quickly. The glucose level in the blood may become low because not enough has been eaten, or because the person takes some extra exercise or because too much insulin has been injected. Similarly the glucose level can become too high because too much has been eaten or not enough insulin has been injected. Diabetics, with the help of their doctors, usually quickly learn the correct balance to suit them. In this way most diabetics can lead normal lives.

WEAR AND TEAR

All too often we expect more from our bodies than they are able to give. For instance we may try to lift a weight which is too heavy, with the result that something in the body has to give. This sort of damage is repairable by the body itself, although often considerable help is necessary. This generally means resting the damaged part until it is healed.

Health problems like these can be thought of as failures of a part, but they are different from the failures described earlier since they are repairable and are often the result of a gradual weakening of a part before it finally gives way.

Slipped disc

A disc is a small wedge of *cartilage* which fits in between the bones of the spine. These bones are called the *vertebrae* and

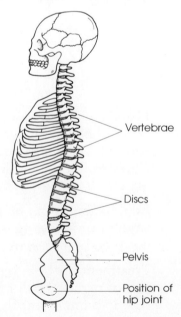

Skeleton cut away to show the discs between the vertebrae of the spine

we have twenty-four of them. This means that there are twenty-four discs. Cartilage is a slippery substance a little bit like polythene in appearance. The discs stop the vertebrae from rubbing and grating against each other, which they would otherwise do since bone is nowhere near as slippery as cartilage.

Each vertebra fits neatly into the one above and below, but to stop them from coming apart from each other they are all joined by *ligaments*. These are tough stretchy sheets of tissue which allow the bones to move about a bit but not too much.

To get a slipped disc, what usually happens is that you put too much strain on your back. This stretches the ligaments just a little too far. A large enough gap occurs on one side of the spinal column for the disc to move out of position.

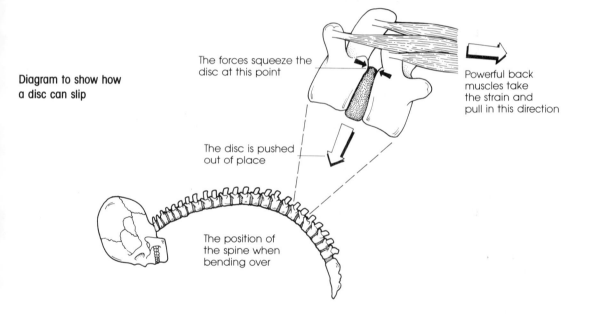

Diagram to show how a disc can slip

The spinal cord, the main nerve in the body, runs through a hole in the centre of the vertebrae. Any shift in position of the vertebrae may cause pressure on the spinal cord. This may cause a most alarming pain, often making you completely immobile — any movement hurts so much that no movement is possible.

The only cure is to try to get the disc back into the correct position and then to allow the ligaments enough time to regain their strength. This may mean lying flat on your back for days or weeks. What often happens is that the stretched ligament and its associated muscles never become quite as strong as they were, and there is a risk that the disc could slip again. Obviously then, it would be wise to take very great care when lifting and stretching.

Ligaments and muscles

Awkward lifting or straining can damage the muscles and ligaments of the back without necessarily causing a slipped disc. Back troubles of this sort are very common. More people have time off work with back trouble than for any other single complaint. Usually the trouble is self-inflicted.

Ligaments are found not only in the back but at every joint in the body. Strain at any joint can cause one to tear. You may have heard of a footballer tearing a ligament through a tackle where his leg gets twisted too far the wrong way.

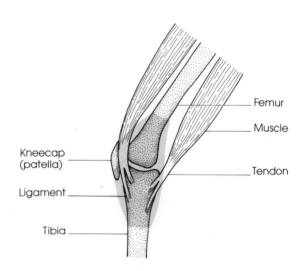

The knee joint showing the arrangement of muscles, tendons and ligaments

In the same way muscle can be torn. A torn muscle may mean the flesh of the muscle is ripped or it may mean that the muscle is torn away from its tendon. Either way total rest is necessary for the muscle to repair itself. The same is true for torn tendons. Usually a torn tendon means that it is ripped away from its normal attachment to the bone, or the tendon itself may actually tear. Torn muscles and tendons are often caused by making the muscle do more work than it should. The muscle produces so much effort that when the bone does not move, something in between breaks. The diagram at the top of the next page shows how these problems could arise if you try to lift too much weight the wrong way.

The wrong and the right way to lift

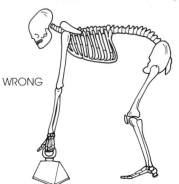
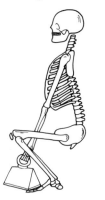

Broken bones

Bones will break, like muscles and ligaments, if too much force is put on them. Luckily they usually mend quite easily and all that is normally necessary is to hold the broken parts together. This is usually done with a plaster cast. Many bones will heal in about 6 weeks, although it takes longer in older people.

How a plaster cast works

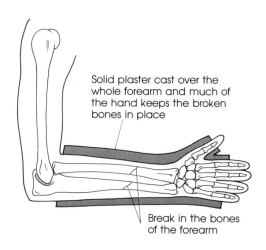

QUESTIONS ON PARTS FAILURE

1 Describe the factors which may lead to a heart attack.
2 Explain how a pacemaker is fitted and what it does.
3 What problems are encountered in a heart transplant?
4 Fill in the spaces in the following sentences. Do not write on this page.

The two kidneys produce the waste liquid____ which is stored in the ____ until it can be removed. A kidney transplant is only necessary when ____ kidneys fail. A kidney machine or ____ machine may be used if a patient cannot have a transplant.

5 What does a dialysis machine do? Under what circumstances will a person need to use a dialysis machine?

6 Explain the common form of diabetes. How can this condition be controlled?

7 What is a disc? Under what conditions will a disc slip? Describe what happens and what can be done about it.

8 Fill in the spaces in the following sentences. Do not write on this page.
Lifting heavy objects the wrong way can lead to a ____ or torn ____, ____ or ____. When lifting correctly the ____ and ____ muscles do the work.

9 Jimmy Johnson plays football for the factory team. He is off work this week with a torn ligament in his leg. How do you think this could have happened? What treatment will Jimmy need?

'HEART TRANSPLANTS'

The 'words' below have all been given 'heart transplants'. This means that the middle letters of a word have been put in the middle of another word. Give them back their correct hearts and then match the real words with the clues below. Do not write on this page.

(a) CHOLDNEROL
(b) DIABESIS
(c) DIACOTES
(d) GLYSULGEN
(e) INUITIN

(f) KICREY
(g) PACLYKER
(h) PANTEBEAS
(i) PITESTARY
(j) VEREMARAE

Clues

1 A fatty substance found in meat.
2 An organ of the body. It removes waste products from the blood.
3 One of the organs which can be transplanted from one person to another. Its name appears on the new donor card.
4 A disease caused by the failure of 10.
5 A machine like this helps people to overcome the effects of a failure of 2.
6 Bones of the spine.
7 A hormone which controls blood sugar level.
8 Glucose is stored as this substance in the body.
9 Name for a patch of tissue at the top of the right atrium.
10 This organ which lies just below the stomach normally manufactures 7.

CHAPTER 8

SOCIAL DISEASES

This is a group of several sorts of disease which all have one thing in common — they are all related to the way we live. They seem, in particular, to be linked with the sort of life-style found in Europe and North America. This is, of course, not strictly true and examples of these diseases can be found anywhere in the world. What is important is that these diseases seem to affect a great many people in the western world and are a great cause for concern. The social diseases are grouped under four headings: smoking, drinking, body weight problems and sexually transmitted diseases.

SMOKING

A great deal has been written about the dangers associated with smoking. Cigarettes are the most harmful because almost always the smoke is inhaled deep into the lungs. Pipe and cigar smokers tend just to retain the smoke in their mouths and therefore do not damage their lungs so much. Those people who do inhale pipe or cigar smoke run greater risks than cigarette smokers, because the smoke from cigars and pipes contains a greater amount of harmful substances.

Cigarette smoke contains:

1) *Tar* — a mixture of a large number of substances, some of which are now known to cause cancer;
2) *Carbon monoxide* — a poisonous gas;
3) *Nicotine* — an addictive drug.

Cigarette smoking damages the body in the following ways:

1) It destroys the delicate lung-cleaning system. Inside the lungs the tiny airways are lined with special cells. These have *cilia* — very small hairs — which wave from side to side and gently sweep a thin layer of mucus out of the lungs. Any dirt and dust which gets into the

lungs is trapped in this mucus layer and swept out. Cigarette smoke poisons these cells and prevents the cilia from working. It also increases the amount of mucus produced causing smoker's cough.

A section through a bronchiole to show the lung-cleaning mechanism

2) Cigarette smoking causes the destruction of the internal surface of the lungs and so reduces the amount of surface available to take in oxygen. The tar and oils stick in the mucus and produce a heavy phlegm which sinks down into the lungs. The body responds by coughing to try to bring this phlegm up. Eventually this 'smoker's cough' causes the lung cells to become damaged and break so that they can no longer take in oxygen. In addition, the damaged lung cells allow other infections to start. Bronchitis is much more common among smokers than non-smokers.

Constant coughing eventually damages lung tissue

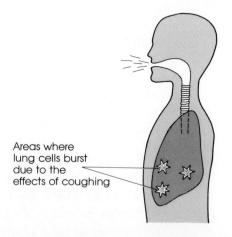

3) Cigarette smoking reduces the blood's ability to carry oxygen. *Haemoglobin* is the substance which carries oxygen from the lungs around the body. Carbon monoxide gas combines with haemoglobin and prevents it from carrying oxygen. This produces strains on the blood system as the heart pumps faster to compensate for the reduced amount of oxygen.

4) Cigarette smoking leads to hardening of the arteries, which puts a strain on the heart and may lead to a heart attack.
5) In pregnant women smoking can be responsible for babies being smaller and possibly less healthy than normal.

Some young people smoke to look grown-up or glamorous

6) Cigarette smoking may lead to lung cancer. It is now well-established that some of the substances in smoke can cause cancer. Unfortunately, when arguing against this, people often point to others who have smoked for years and not developed lung cancer. This is true; not everyone who smokes will get this disease. Smoking does, however, vastly increase the risk and it is not possible to predict who will get it and who will not. Since you cannot check to make sure that you will not get lung cancer, would *you* take the risk? You should realise that lung cancer is almost unknown in non-smokers.
7) Finally, not a health risk but a social problem — smokers smell. They smell of stale cigarettes. A non-smoker can always detect a smoker by the smell. Not only does a smoker's breath smell, but also their clothes, their room, their car, all take on the smell of an old ashtray. The smoker, of course, never notices, but more and more non-smokers are objecting. In public places like cinemas and trains, smokers are having to sit in certain places to reduce their effects on other people.

Why smoke? There are many answers to this question. Some people get real pleasure from smoking. Probably the vast majority of adults smoke because they cannot give up the habit. Only you can decide whether to smoke or not. Before you try smoking, look at the many reasons why you should not smoke. How many reasons are there why you should?

DRINKING

People have been drinking alcoholic drinks for many centuries. It is probably true that for a long time it was much safer to drink wine or beer than it was to drink water. There is enough alcohol in wine to prevent the growth of many microbes which could cause disease. Similarly, beer is made by boiling the malt liquid with hops. The boiling would kill many microbes and the hops, too, are known to kill some bacteria.

Drinking, then, was part of everyday life for many people, so why is it now a problem? The first point to realise is that alcohol is a drug and a poison. Even in small amounts it slows down the working of the nervous system. The body can deal with small amounts of alcohol, but larger quantities, for example the amounts in one to two pints of beer, quickly bring changes to the nervous system.

A frequent early change is a relaxation of inhibitions. At parties or at the pub many people find it easier to talk to others and enjoy themselves. It does not really matter much if they talk a little too loudly or act a bit silly. What often happens is that this relaxation makes people want to drink a little more because they feel good. This leads to them becoming more drunk. Speech becomes slurred and they sway a little as they walk. Vision, too, may become blurred and reactions are a lot slower than normal.

Drinking always slows your reactions and impairs your vision

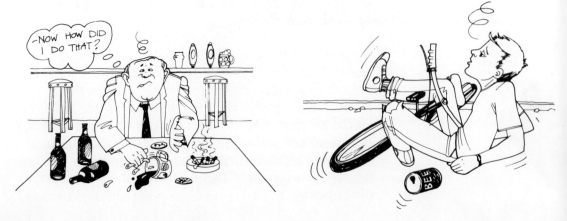

Even this may not be a disaster until perhaps they decide to drive home. Reactions are so much slower that a person like this is totally unfit to ride even a bicycle. It does not take much alcohol to get to this state, which is why in the United Kingdom the legal limit for drivers is 80 mg of alcohol per 100 cm^3 of blood. This is now measured as 35 mg of alcohol in 100 cm^3 of breath and represents about two pints of beer or two whiskies.

Drunk people, too, show strange reactions. Small incidents may upset them for no reason. This often leads to fighting, with the fighters having no real control over what they are doing.

Drinking beyond this stage is not a pleasure and yet some people continue to do it. Eventually the nervous system becomes so dulled that the person passes out. The brain gives up for a while to allow the body time to recover. This is a good thing since further drinking would probably cause death. *Remember: alcohol is a poison.*

Regular drinkers may find that they begin to depend on that slightly drunk, relaxed state. They find that they cannot face life without regular small drinks. Such people are *alcoholics.* They are ill and need help. Usually the alcoholic does not realise their need for drink and so help is very difficult to give. Alcoholism is responsible for a good deal of sadness in today's world. Marriages break up, and children go hungry or without proper clothing when the household money is used to buy drink.

Drinking moderate amounts, then, can be enjoyable and probably does no harm. Drunkenness, however, is never pleasant. It should not be encouraged either by you or your friends. At best you get a hangover, at worst, it can lead to death, possibly of someone else. And remember: regular drinking can lead to alcoholism.

OBESITY AND ANOREXIA

These are the opposite extremes of the problem of body weight. Obesity is the problem of being grossly overweight by having too much fat. Anorexia, or more correctly anorexia nervosa, is a condition where a person diets so severely that they lose weight to the point of putting their life in danger.

Being overweight is one of the most worrying problems in the western world. It seems that when there is plenty to eat many people eat too much. People who are obese eat too much of the wrong foods. It must be pointed out, however,

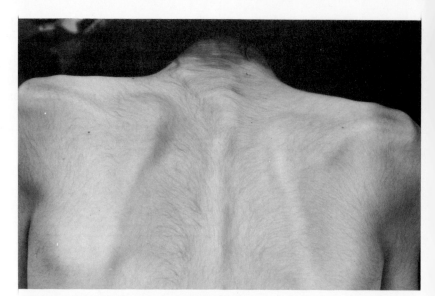

Severe dieting causes anorexia

Over-eating causes obesity

that not all large people are obese. People may vary a lot in their size. To give you some idea of the variation, look at the table. This gives you the possible normal body weights for teenagers in the age range 15 to 19. Because of the way young people grow it is not really possible to give weight ranges for youngsters of less than 15 years.

Weight range in Indoor Clothing

(Reproduced by permission of Northampton Health Education Department)

	Height Ft In	*15–19 years* Pounds		*Height* Ft In	*15–19 years* Pounds
Boys	6 2	146–182	*Girls*	5 11	135–168
	6 1	141–176		5 10	131–163
	6 0	137–171		5 9	126–158
	5 11	132–165		5 8	122–153
	5 10	128–159		5 7	119–149
	5 9	123–154		5 6	115–144
	5 8	120–149		5 5	112–140
	5 7	116–145		5 4	108–135
	5 6	113–140		5 3	104–131
	5 5	109–136		5 2	102–127
	5 4	105–131		5 1	99–122
	5 3	102–127		5 0	96–120
	5 2	99–124		4 11	94–117
	5 1	96–120		4 10	92–115
	5 0	94–117		4 9	91–114
				4 8	90–113

(1 ft = 30 cm; 2.2 lb = 1 kg)

People become obese for many reasons. Some people work all day sitting down. They eat and drink too much and take little exercise. Slowly they put on weight until one day they discover that some of their old clothes do not fit. They may no longer be capable of any sort of exercise. They get out of breath easily if they try to run. Some people get bored or depressed and eat to cheer themselves up. This may often happen to women who are at home all day. Whatever the cause these people get too fat. This can lead to heart problems, high blood pressure, diabetes and other conditions. It can also increase the risk of suffering from gallstones, osteoarthritis and varicose veins. In addition it makes you feel and look less attractive.

The only cure is to eat less and exercise more. It is not necessary, or even advisable, to go on a crash diet. Just work the fat off gradually, the same way as you put it on. Remember: the earlier a person becomes obese, then the greater the risks to life in the years 40 to 60.

Anorexia is a condition found most commonly among teenage girls. They seem to become so obsessed with the idea that they are overweight that they simply stop eating. If they have to have a meal, they may stick their fingers down their throat to make themselves vomit it up again. This vomiting can eventually become an automatic reaction and even uncontrollable, which is why anorexia can become life-threatening. The causes of anorexia are not fully understood. They must in some way be linked to society's preoccupation with weight. It would seem that the ideal body to have is one which is slim and trim. Advertisements make a great deal of this but not everybody can look like a model. You must accept that, provided your diet is balanced and you do not eat too much, then you are the way you are. People with anorexia do not seem to be able to accept this.

Nowadays anorexia is recognised as a medical condition and should be treated by a doctor.

SEXUALLY TRANSMITTED DISEASES (STD)

These are diseases which are transferred from person to person during sexual intercourse. They affect the reproductive organs, although they may spread to other parts of the body. There are four main common sexually transmitted diseases:

1) *Syphilis,* caused by bacteria
2) *Gonorrhoea,* caused by bacteria
3) *Non-specific urethritis* (NSU), caused by bacteria
4) *Herpes genitalis,* caused by a virus.

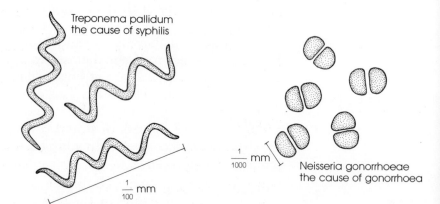

The bacteria which cause STD

Two other common sexually transmitted diseases are *thrush,* caused by a fungus, and *trichomoniasis vaginalis* (TV), caused by a protozoan.

Away from the body, the organisms which cause the veneral diseases quickly die. It is therefore unlikely that you will catch STD by anything other than sexual intercourse. Treatment for these diseases is usually simple but must be done by a doctor. This can be either your own doctor, or a doctor at the special clinic of a hospital. There are no home cures for STD and so if you suspect you may have it then you must see a doctor. You can find the address of the special clinic by looking in the telephone directory, under the heading Venereal Disease (VD), or by simply telephoning the casualty department of the local hospital and asking.

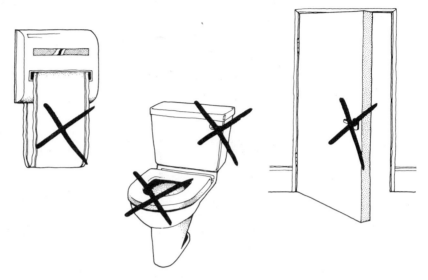

You DON'T catch STD from these

Treatment either by your doctor or at the special clinic is completely confidential. You will have to give your name and address and also the names and addresses of anyone you have had intercourse with recently. This will allow the doctor to trace the disease and treat it in people who may not even know they have it. Despite these precautions STD is on the increase, especially among young people and there is a great risk that people who have casual sex will eventually catch one of the sexually transmitted diseases.

Syphilis

In males the symptoms are a painless sore on the penis. In females this sore is inside the vagina and is also painless. It may therefore go unnoticed. In any case the sore will disappear of its own accord in a couple of weeks. Untreated syphilis spreads throughout the body and may eventually lead to heart disease, brain disease, blindness and finally death. Pregnant women can pass syphilis to their babies, in whom it causes severe abnormalities.

Gonorrhoea

In males the symptoms are a burning sensation when urinating and a yellow smelly discharge which drips out of the penis. In females the disease may go unnoticed. It may, however, produce pain when urinating and she may notice an unusual discharge. Untreated gonorrhoea often leads to infection of the reproductive system which can eventually make the sufferer sterile. Gonorrhoea, too, can pass from a pregnant woman to her baby as it is being born, causing infection of the eyes.

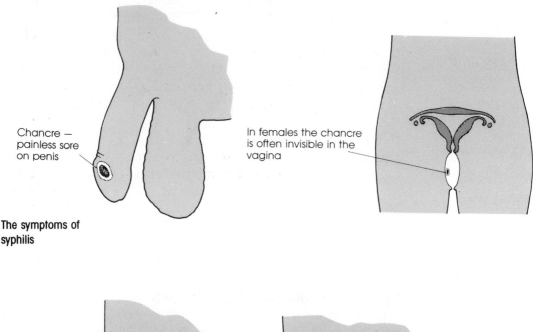

The symptoms of syphilis

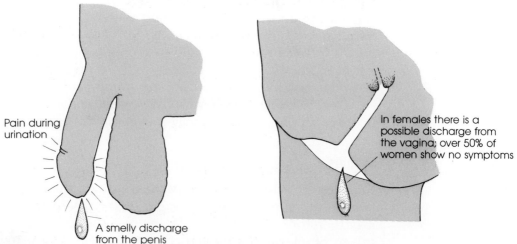

The symptoms of gonorrhoea

Non-specific urethritis

In males this produces a pain during urination and often a smelly discharge from the penis. In females there are often no symptoms at all and so women are the carriers of this disease. Untreated NSU can lead to arthritis, eye infection and larger infections of the reproductive organs, which may cause females to become sterile.

Herpes genitalis

This is caused by the same type of virus that causes cold sores. Its symptoms are sores on the penis or the edge of the vagina. Since it is caused by a virus it cannot be treated by antibiotics and is therefore almost incurable. Treatment includes relieving the discomfort caused by the sores until the body is able to heal itself. If untreated the sores may become infected by other organisms. Because of the difficulty of treating herpes, the disease may flare up again after the symptoms have subsided with treatment. The virus lies dormant and reappears when conditions seem to favour it. Once caught, a person will carry this virus for life.

Remember: if you suspect that you may have caught a sexually transmitted disease, then you must go to a doctor. Only in this way can it accurately be diagnosed and, if necessary, treated. You should realise, too, that even if you have been cured of such a disease you can catch it again. The only sure way to avoid it is to avoid casual sex.

QUESTIONS ON SOCIAL DISEASES

1 What is the addictive drug in cigarettes? What does addictive mean?

2 What harm does the tar in cigarette smoke do?

3 How can smoking damage your lungs?

4 What diseases are smokers more likely to suffer from than non-smokers?

5 List the reasons why people smoke. Now list the reasons why they should not.

6 What can smoking do to an unborn baby?

7 What effects does drinking have on vision and speed of reactions?

8 Why does drinking make some people miserable and aggresive but makes others happy?

9 What is the maximum amount of alcohol you can have in your blood and still be legally able to drive? How much beer or whisky is this equivalent to? Why is there this legal limit?

10 What is an alcoholic?

11 What is obesity? How do people become obese?

12 What can obese people do to help their weight problem?

13 What is anorexia? What sort of person is most likely to suffer from it?

14 Name the common sexually transmitted diseases and list the symptoms for each one.

15 Explain why males are more likely to realise they have STD than females.

16 How do you get treatment for STD? What questions will the doctor ask?

17 Can you catch STD more than once?

WORDFINDER ON SOCIAL DISEASES

Trace the wordfinder on to a piece of paper. Then solve the following clues and put a ring around the answers. Answers go in any direction: across, back, up, down and diagonally. The answer to Question 1 is ringed already to give you a start.

A	R	P	O	I	S	O	N
E	N	I	T	O	C	I	N
T	H	O	A	R	T	E	S
A	N	E	R	V	O	S	A
L	A	E	R	E	N	E	V
U	B	E	E	P	X	S	E
N	F	A	G	T	E	I	D
G	H	C	E	E	P	S	A

1 Cigarette smoke contains _____ (3) . . .

2 . . . and _____ (8) . . .

3 . . . and may damage _____ cells (4)

4 Alcohol is a _____ (6) . . .

5 . . . and it can make your _____ slurred (6)

6 A sensible _____ may help you slim (4) . . .

7, 8 . . . but be careful to avoid the condition called _____ _____ (7, 8: 2 words in separate places)

9 The V of VD stands for _____ (8)

10 One form of STD is _____ genitalis (6)

ANSWERS TO WORDFINDERS

Tapeworm wordfinder p. 6

Worm 1   Worm 2
Lungs   Muscles
Brain   Oxygen
Food   Protein
Water   Heart
Fat   Meals
Vitamins

Wordfinder on microbes p. 14

1 Cells
2 Antibodies
3 Microbes
4 Virus
5 Bacteria
6 Toxin
7 Antigens
8 Aspirin
9 White
10 Phagocyte
11 Polio
12 Blood

Wordfinder on cancer p. 47

Danger, Government Health Warning, cigarettes can seriously damage your health.

Wordfinder on social diseases p. 72

1 Tar
2 Nicotine
3 Lung
4 Poison
5 Speech
6 Diet
7, 8 Anorexia nervosa
9 Venereal
10 Herpes

INDEX

Alcohol 64, 65
Anorexia 65
Antibiotic 11
Antibody 9, 12

Bacteria 7, 9, 10, 68
Balanced diet 2
Bedbugs 21
Blackhead 26
Broken bones 59

Carbohydrate 2
Carcinogen 43, 44
Cartilage 56, 57
Cholesterol 49
Comedo 26

Dialysis 53

Fats 2
Flea 18
Fungi 7, 17

Gonorrhoea 68, 69

Head lice 19
Heart attack 48, 63
Heart transplant 50, 60
Herpes 68, 71
Hormone 25, 36

Insulin 54, 55

Kidney machine 53
Kidney transplant 54

Lice 17

Ligament 57, 58
Lung cancer 44, 47, 63

Microbe 3, 7
Mineral 2
Mite 20

Nicotine 61
Nits 19
Non-specific urethritis 68, 70

Obesity 50, 65

Pacemaker 51
Parasite 4, 18
Protein 2
Protozoa 7

Scabies 20
Scanner 46
Sebum 23, 25
Slipped disc 56
Smoking 50, 61
Syphilis 68, 69

Toxins 3, 8
Tumour 42, 43
   benign 42
   malignant 42

Vertebra 56, 57
Virus 7, 11, 16
Vitamin 2

White blood cell 8
Whitehead 26

X-rays 45, 46